Shakespeare's Political Animal

Shakespeare's Political Animal

Schema and Schemata in the Canon

Alan Hager

Newark: University of Delaware Press
London and Toronto: Associated University Presses

© 1990 by Associated University Presses, Inc.

All rights reserved. Authorization to photocopy items for internal or personal use, or the internal or personal use of specific clients, is granted by the copyright owner, provided that a base fee of $10.00, plus eight cents per page, per copy is paid directly to the Copyright Clearance Center, 27 Congress Street, Salem, Massachusetts 01970. [0-87413-371-8/90 $10.00 + 8¢ pp, pc.]

Associated University Presses
440 Forsgate Drive
Cranbury, NJ 08512

Associated University Presses
25 Sicilian Avenue
London WC1A 2QH, England

Associated University Presses
P.O. Box 488, Port Credit
Mississauga, Ontario
Canada L5G 4M2

The paper used in this publication meets the requirements of the American National Standard for Permanence of Paper for Printed Library Materials Z39.48-1984.

Library of Congress Cataloging-in-Publication Data

Hager, Alan.
  Shakespeare's political animal : schema and schemata in the canon / Alan Hager.
    p. cm.
  Includes bibliographical references.
  ISBN 0-87413-371-8 (alk. paper)
  1. Shakespeare, William, 1564–1616—Political and social views. 2. Politics in literature. I. Title.
PR3017.H3   1990
822.3'3—dc20   88-40585
                                                                  CIP

PRINTED IN THE UNITED STATES OF AMERICA

To Carol and Stephen

Contents

Preface 9
Acknowledgments 15

Part 1. Benevolent Deception and Rule
1 The Concept of the Machiavellian Ruler of Sonnet 94 and Its Discontents 21
2 Teaching the Sly Animal to Be Civil: *The Taming of the Shrew* as Shakespeare's Anatomy of Education 26
3 From Hal to Henry V: The Deceptive Ruler and His Discontents 34

Part 2. Leveling, through Rivalry and Victimization
4 "Remorse in Myself with His Words": Shakespeare's Schematic Picture of Factional Behavior 41
5 "The Teeth of Emulation": Failed Sacrifice in Shakespeare's *Julius Caesar* 51

Part 3. The Politics of Literary Borrowing and Exclusion
6 Publishing the Politics of Literary Expropriation: Lyly and Marlowe in *1 Henry IV* 67
7 Exorcizing the Moral Jonsonian Citizen Comedy in Shakespeare's *Twelfth Night, or, What You Will* 76
8 Sacrificing the Mysteries: Dismembering the Text in Early Criticism of Shakespeare's *Julius Caesar* 88

Part 4. Self-Destructive Tyranny in Oligarchy and Monarchy
9 England's Sicily and Shakespeare's Critique of Gallantry in *Much Ado about Nothing* 97
10 What Rusts the Soul: Shakespeare's *Macbeth* and the Invention of the Conscience 105

Part 5. Ideal Solutions and Their Discontents
11 Shakespeare's Critique of the Mirage of the Green World in *As You Like It* and *The Winter's Tale* 117

12	Hierarchy and Freedom in the New World: Duke Prospero's Education in the Yare	127

Epilogue: Ulysses' Political Thoughts and Action in Reverse — 135

Notes — 139
Bibliography — 153
Index — 159

Preface

At one point, early in Shakespeare's great Roman play, Brutus, hearing his fellow conspirators knock on the door, speaks of the horror—"like a phantasma or a hideous dream" (2.1.65)[1]—present in his soul in anticipation of the murder of his friend and *imperator*, Julius Caesar. He says of his nightmarish internal condition that

> The genius and the mortal instruments
> Are then in council, and the state of a man,
> Like to a little kingdom, suffers then
> The nature of an insurrection.
>
> (2.1.66–69)

Oddly with his angst about control and oppression and his loss of freedom to deliberate decisions on a par in Rome—above all, about the possibility of a new *rex*—Brutus here seems anxious to maintain a regal chain of command within his own being.

What explains the terror of Brutus's nightmarish discovery but the notion of an internal absence of rule, or leveling? The attendant spirit, the "genius" of the soul, its king, finds himself not holding to a position of command that would make him perhaps a "charismatic" leader, controlling lieutenants through regal self-image and style, but in doubtful deliberation with his own subjects, the "mortal instruments," that is, the emotional and intellective faculties of his being. Brutus does not seem to fear democracy in his soul exactly, but a general loss of rank, an anarchy, an absence of ruler that produces the opposite of "kingdom." All elements of his inner self are equal, and that condition amounts to an insurrection, a simultaneous uprising and self-lowering that leads to bad dreams, and thus insomnia.

In a healthy soul, feelings and thoughts, "the mortal instruments," apparently hold to their inferior position as deputies and do not usurp themselves. Brutus, however, pictures a ghostly image of all sensory, cognitive, and emotional lieutenants suddenly promoted to natural general. The "general" mass of subjects becomes the "general" or absolute authority in his waking nightmare. As so often in the play, Brutus, apparently unknowingly, parodies and thus condemns the conspiracy of senators that puts itself, in a crisis of rule in Rome, on equal footing with the *imperator*, Julius Caesar. This political uprising, as Brutus gradually learns, leads not only to Caesar's death, but also to the demise of all leading conspirators, and of many others, too, often at random. "Equalizing" leads to the chaos and destruction implied by the modern sense of the term. "With himself at war" (1.2.46), he glimpses the worst. David Bevington says that the "conflict between idealistic principles and sordid conspiracy produces in Brutus a fatal division of personality; the gentle friend of Caesar and the assassin cannot understand one another."[2] Brutus's internal confusion, however, also grows out of a "rank" disorder he glimpses in his own soul, and its action suggests a theory of monarchic rule, not unfamiliar to Shakespeare's first audience.

Although the Elizabethans reveled in personal freedom guaranteed in the Magna Carta, the English constitution, and their parliamentary system,[3] they normally looked at politics in terms of the gestalt of monarch and subjects. In general, autocratic systems were conceived to be perfectible, and if they fail, one must look for a number of causes. Tyrants or the tyranny of mobs in the cities, for example, may not even be the major cause of a failed monarchy. When Elizabeth's ambassador to Russia, Giles Fletcher the Elder, sets out to define endemic trouble in the Muscovite commonwealth, taken to be a tyranny, one may expect to hear of monarchic malfeasance and factional overreaction, but for Fletcher, the elementary disease in rule results—as it did for many Elizabethan thinkers[4]—not from excess of authority in king or tribune, but from a loss of hierarchical identity, or rank, in the ruler. This political condition creates a situation where magistrates fill a vacuum of power and victimize the poor people of the realm.

Warnings throughout the late Tudor period about the dangers of Elizabeth's own potential retirement from office attest not only to a nearly universal acceptance of the conceptual framework of England's hereditary system of rule, but also to a concept that a default of power of the ruler may pose the greatest danger to the health of England's political system. Whatever the inconsistencies of Gaunt's idealized picture of Old England, it should remain for him, a "scept'red isle, / This earth of majesty" (2.1.40), a "royal throne of kings," even if then, as he saw it, it "preys upon itself" (2.1.39).[5] Star chambers, appellate courts, houses of lords and commons, and magistrates all ideally provide conduits, not checks, for monarchic authority, but the system can attract a variety of diseases whose complex syndromes—most notably, leveling—require sophisticated remedies.

Schematically, this monarchic conceptualization of the nature of rule enjoyed the advantage of compatibility with the theological macrocosm of God and the universe of good and bad angels and men. Authorities could fashion rebellious subjects in terms of Luciferian faction, as they often did, especially in sermons of the era,[6] and speak of the healthiness of unwavering Godlike rule. Furthermore, kingly tyrannical behavior could be compared unfavorably to that of an imaged deity, unswayed by flatterers, making ultimately beneficent decisions through His inscrutable prescience and vitality. Under the influence of Machiavelli and others,[7] in fact, Renaissance political theoreticians developed a concept that the good ruler, like God, had to allow or even create what appeared to be evil for an ultimate good that shortsighted and ultimately perverse subjects were likely to misconstrue. In this case the ruler works through deception. The notion of the contrived mysteries of rule applied, of course, not only to the universe, to the state, but also to Aristotle's political atom, the family, and to the microcosm, the human soul itself, as in Brutus's ominous self-scrutiny. The "genius" must rule and be misunderstood—intentionally.

This extreme autocratic concept suggests its own antinomy in the notion of the fever or plague of leveling, a contagious disease of nonrule Shakespeare dwells on, even morbidly. He compares it in play and poem to eclipse, or other astronomical disorder, earthquake and fire in the natural universe, leading to promiscuous death. Leveling lacks all contrivance, for it causes a brutalization of man, now a fellow to the animals, no longer *rationis capax*. Nonrule produces an absence of inscrutable "majestic" position, creating a vacuum that draws into the body politic a free-for-all of rival factions, what René Girard has called, in another context, "undifferentiation"[8] that leads to the reemergence of savage custom, of imposed indifference, and of scapegoat spectacle. Shakespeare's Marcius says to the unruly citizens in Rome, for example, echoing Gaunt, that without rule they "would feed on one another" (1.1.183), or they would focus their energy on random victims. The process of political breakdown in the universe, state, family, or, as I have suggested, in the microcosm of Brutus's soul, can lead to a savage condition where rivalry reigns, symbolized, in its last stage, by cannibalism and human sacrifice.

Such a system of monarchic principles—and emergency valves—may prove discordant for the modern ear, but the processes are hardly unfamiliar. In the freest or most democratic society, one recognizes the necessary presence of hierarchy at business and play, and the dangers concomitant to its failure. I feel, however, that the supreme Elizabethan poets, dramatists, theologians, and political scientists dwell most intensively on the problem of rule and leveling, in part, because of England's recent history of internal disorder, of botched succession and civil disturbance in the streets of London. Sir Philip Sidney, Edmund Spenser, Christopher Marlowe, John Lyly, Samuel Daniel, Francis Bacon, and others—admittedly often responding to censors and royal wishes—keyed political, dramatic, and philosophical works to the problem of rule and the hazards of misrule: uncontrolled rivalry, leveling, and arbitrary singling out victims on the basis of visibility. But Tudor consolidation of power cannot fully explain the popularity of this idea and its rigorous representation on the stage. It constituted a leading idea of the era.

Recent criticism in the 1980s, sometimes of a "new historical" or "iconoclastic" bent,[9] has emphasized self-contradiction and paradox in Shakespeare's representations of political processes, reflecting the Stratford dramatist's own compliance and struggle with authority and images of power in his society. Jonathon Dollimore, for example, has recently suggested that the attempt to discover a picture of "'man's' essential nature"[10] in Shakespeare's representation of the "political animal" is critical self-deception, in part, on the grounds that the dialectic of history contradicts the idea of man's unchanging nature. Moreover, Stephen Greenblatt concludes his brilliant work on "Renaissance self-fashioning"—and Dollimore echoes him—with the observation that "the human subject," including Shakespeare, "began to seem remarkably unfree, the ideological product of the relations of power in a particular society."[11] *Ethnos* not *ethos*, they argue, binds Shakespeare's thought. The playwright, they say, must respond to specific exertions of authority, rather than conceptualize, in a consistent way, its working. Although my conclusions are often similar to those of Greenblatt and other "new historicists," even borrowing some of their methods, I arrive at them from a different angle, from a search for precision and continuity, not ignoring, of course, the traces of internal disorder.

Recently, in rejecting his early notion of the "totalizing" society and the "total" artist, Shakespeare, Greenblatt says that "even those literary texts that sought most ardently to speak for a monolithic power could be shown to be the sites of institutional and ideological contestation."[12] Certainly Shakespeare represented the state that, in a sense, published him with surprisingly "contested" results, most notably in the texts of *King Lear*, as Annabel Patterson and Richard Strier have shown.[13] I argue, however, that Shakespeare's theory of political behavior, exploded or not, even in *King Lear*, remains remarkably free of the signs of coercion and rebellion. Furthermore, if Shakespeare's conceptualization of the human as political animal admits paradox, I argue it is not the self-contradiction of an "ardent" iconoclast, but that of a critic of life taking apart and reassembling what he took to be a constant: human nature. As Girard, James Siemon, and, to some extent, Stephen Booth, conclude, Shakespeare has already deconstructed himself. One of my jobs as critic is to discover how.

Whatever the dictates of historical process, Shakespeare seems ultimately self-consistent in his picture of human nature in its political success and failure, not only within the realm of specific plays, but throughout his career. This book argues for Shakespearean consonance in what Sidney calls the "*idea* or foreconceit"[14] of his works from beginning to end. Many of his poems and plays, early and late, I argue, reveal a design that suggests (1) systematic investigation of the nature of his political animal on the right or wrong assumption that human genius is free enough to alter history and historical process for good or ill, and (2) that human nature does not change, to paraphrase Aristotle's *Ethics* 5.7, "as fire burns both here and in Persia."[15] Shakespeare structures some of his works in and around specific problems of rule, rivalry, leveling, and victimization. Nonrule, of tyrant and mob, as he pictures it, has no easy solution. If it has not reached an advanced stage, it can disappear with the reestablishment of the identity of the participants. If acute, it gropes toward order only through destruction of the ruler, or, in fact, anyone or anything, now or formerly, of distinction. Only on that sad note can a once doomed society begin to rebuild itself. Only then can the plague-ridden island world be "civilized" anew.

Shakespeare's apparent principles of rule and leveling, I argue, apply not only to his poetic and dramatic constructs but to the highly self-conscious and "politicized" ambience of literary rivalry and criticism in his day and following, suggested most notably in his relationship to his competing masters of the stage—Kyd, Lyly, Marlowe, Greene, and, above all, Ben Jonson. Thus, my study opens with Shakespearean images of beneficent deception of rulers, moving to those of leveling, then to those which reflect the arena of poetic competition. I then demonstrate Shakespeare's pictures of oligarchic and monarchic disorder, and his representations of the beauty and failure of ideal solutions. Peculiarly, Shakespeare "refutes" the assumptions of some of his twentieth-century polemical readers in his "criticism" of idealists in general. Ideals, in Shakespeare, apparently cannot alter what he takes to be the political condition of human nature, but form an essential part of it. High aspirations are aims, in the word's basic sense, necessarily an overshooting, always gloriously human, but never divine. Throughout his career as a poet and playwright, he dramatizes the Icaran nature of schemes of perfectibility, which provide the only motivation to personal and social good of man the political animal. My short epilogue looks at the deceiver Ulysses' deconstruction and reconstruction of a notion of political process.

That Shakespeare appears to be ultimately optimistic about political solutions—even in relation to his rival poets—reflects, I argue, not only his apparent glimpses of monarchic beneficence in the universe—most notable in his late plays but seen throughout his opus—but also his position or place as the protector of elementary distinctions, of the most powerful poetic words. Even in the mirror worlds of horror in *Julius Caesar* and *Macbeth*, Shakespeare allows the design of his plays to suggest solution. But then the poet necessarily conserves distinctions. Without them there would be no words, and his trade would be extinct.

Acknowledgments

In the development of this monograph, I have received helpful comments in discussion, correspondence, and review from a mass of thoughtful readers and listeners including Janet Adelman, William S. Anderson, David Bergeron, David Bevington, Gary Bouchard, the late Bertrand Bronson, Claus P. Buechmann, Maria Cordero, Jack D'Amico, Stanley Fish, René Girard, Sandor Goodhart, Suzanne Gossett, Tim Gray, Stephen Greenblatt, Robert Grudin, Clarke Hulse, the late Catherine Jarrott, Arthur Kinney, Connie Brown Kuriyama, Anthony LaBranche, Martin Laub, Mary Lamb, David Loewenstein, Joseph Loewenstein, Roy R. Male, Bernard McElroy, Ruth McGugan, Stephen Orgel, Annabel Patterson, Norman Rabkin, Florence Sandler, Ronald Schleifer, William E. Slights, Rolf Soellner, Patricia Meyer Spacks, Richard Strier, David Sweet, Dain Trafton, Ray Waddington, Andrew Weiner, the late Daniel Wilson, James Yoch, and an array of mystery readers, who read all or part of the manuscript at various stages.

The Sixteenth Century Studies Conference and the Central Renaissance Conferences and their subscribers provided a lively arena for the airing of more than half the chapters in embryo. Efforts in Research Services of Loyola University of Chicago, notably of Tom Bennett, Tim Austin, and Sheila Honda, kept me solvent, in supply, and on course through some hard times. Wende Anderson of the Cudahy library gave me timely aid on more than a few occasions. Janet Lochren and the staff at the Shoreham–Wading River Public Library kept me on keel in the summer.

The Newberry Library, where nearly all the work was drafted and revised, provided unique resources. I would especially like to thank Richard H. Brown, Paul Gehl, Mary Wylie, Mary Beth Rose, John Long, and Karen Skubisch of various departments of that great library for their help.

Two portions of this book previously appeared in print in collections of essays. In a very different and highly polemical form, chapter 9, "The Mirage of the Green World," appeared in *Transitions to Leisure: Conceptual and Human Issues*, edited by B. G. Gunter, Jay Stanley, and Robert St. Clair; in a similar form, chapter 5, "The Teeth of Emulation," appeared in *The Upstart Crow* 8 (1988).

The late Sheldon Allman and his wife, Joan Allman, prepared the manuscript with great skill and patience. Jay Halio, Elizabeth Reynolds, and Kate McKinley of the University of Delaware Press gave me invaluable and timely assistance, as did Julien Yoseloff and Lauren Lepow of the Associated University Presses, as well as my energetic editor, Ronald Roth and, above all, my generous outside reader. Finally, my wife, Carol Burke—to whom, with my two-year-old son, I dedicate this work—provided perpetual encouragement and an editorial eye that would not quit.

Shakespeare's Political Animal

PART 1
Benevolent Deception and Rule

1
The Concept of the Machiavellian Ruler of Sonnet 94 and Its Discontents

> They that have pow'r to hurt and will do none,
> That do not do the thing they most do show,
> Who, moving others, are themselves as stone,
> Unmovèd, cold, and to temptation slow;
> They rightly do inherit heaven's graces
> And husband nature's riches from expense;
> They are the lords and owners of their faces,
> Others but stewards of their excellence.
> The summer's flow'r is to the summer sweet,
> Though to itself it only live and die;
> But if that flow'r with base infection meet,
> The basest weed outbraves his dignity:
>   For sweetest things turn sourest by their deeds;
>   Lilies that fester smell far worse than weeds.

Most readers deal with the apparent impersonality of Shakespeare's sonnet 94 by reading the poem—normally in tandem with excoriating sonnets 93 or 95—as ironically personal in some extreme degree.[1] L. C. Knights, in his marvelous argument about the sonnets, states openly that sonnet 94's "irony is serious and destructive," yet he speaks of its opening as being "coldly analytic (I at least am unable to detect any symptoms of moral fervour)."[2] Stephen Booth hears "the speaker's indecision"[3] but then notes the poem's many "difficulties"[4] as largely intellective, not emotional. I hear no indecision, but rather an emphatic juxtaposition of ideas seemingly designed to surprise Shakespeare's reader. On the basis of this heard tonal "clue," I would like to lift this haikulike abstract-contemplation-fused-to-natural-image from its immediate context and look at it from the perspective of white Machiavellian political doctrine. I insist the poem comprehends this aspect, but I do not deny the plausibility of a personal context as well. Shakespeare was rarely undramatic. From my "impersonal" angle, suddenly, I discover an explanation of political "charisma" and the notion of the anointed ruler, above all, the need for benevolent deception in rulers, all the while hearing of the concomitant internal risks that such deceivers must run. I argue this reading by means of extended metaphrase and paraphrase, exemplification and other forms of amplification:

> They that have pow'r to hurt and will do none,

Who can surely create injury—indeed, who is licensed to injure—but the ruler? The good governor, quite possibly hereditary, will wield his or her strength for public ameliorization, to the detriment of some, and, it is hoped, the advantage of many. In the inevitable "injury" of rule, the good prince will want ("will") no damage to the larger mass of dwellers in the domain. This ruler will try to ("will to") remain on the side of the greater good.

> That do not do the thing they most do show,

Office requires ceremonious deception. Those in authority must use tact with enemies; indeed, they must appear provisionally to be potential allies. They attend church and temple regardless of their own religious feeling. They smile in hospitals and appear generally content with the exigencies of office. But they also employ less clear-cut sorts of necessary deception. The "thing" that is shown (and its tendency) is simply not done in the clear way implied by their action.

> Who, moving others, are themselves as stone,

When they wish to incite the populace, for example, careful timing and other contrived maneuvers become so essential that apparent emotional action must be performed in cold blood. This "inhuman" self-control suggests a metaphoric heart and liver that is not even animate—mere rock. Such "flinty" manipulation of self-image, so good for the state, may not, of course, be good for the ruler's own person, who remains more than "stoic" for an external cause:

> Unmovèd, cold, and to temptation slow;

Temptation itself, in the form of the seductions of the outer world, or of the inner world of imagination and fancy, must have no quick or lively effect on such a ruler. Like a rock, he or she is not movable, freezing cold.

Clearly toward the close of this quatrain, the difficulties of representing the best interests—the greater good—of a body politic have gradually become, in Shakespeare's words, personally onerous, suffocating for the sovereign. This requisite conscious pretender, in the practice of power for the good, must remain so straight as to have no emotional life of his or her own, no thought or feeling that is not part of a design of state.

> They rightly do inherit heaven's graces

The reader, I feel, is initially asked to misread this line and the following one in terms of the theological concept of "grace" as opposed to "nature." This false scent will suggest the high seriousness of the issue of benevolent deception. The continuity of purely political doctrine, however, eventually overwhelms the other sense, but the statement retains a theological implication. The sovereign—with the connotation of hereditary ruler—becomes a little god within his state, creating inscrutable turmoil for his "interested" subjects, like God, for the greater good of the larger number, born and unborn, as far as he or she can see. As a version of the deity, he or she enjoys "heaven's graces" by position and inscrutable presence. In fact, by extension of this idea, like the deity, he or she must, on occasion, allow war, as God allows plague, fire, or flood.

> And husband nature's riches from expense;

The sonnet here moves beyond a theological concept of nature or state of sin to the political fact of usable natural resources of the sublunary state, animal, vegetable, and mineral. The ruler must ration treasures of the natural domain in order to maintain the health of the realm—its ecology. As in Marcius's Rome, if not by natural inclination, then by the exigencies of rivalry and strife, "interested" subjects would always be greedy and squander sheep, grain, or gold. Rulers function, in part, to "check" such waste.

> They are the lords and owners of their faces,

Rulers overlord their own appearance. Their life of controlled image-making requires a kind of secondhand—even self-ironic—

approach to life, which creates a sense of their own "charisma" or magical charm among the populace. The indirection creates, perversely, a necessary fascination.

> Others but stewards of their excellence.

"Steward" suggests a servant in the hierarchy and also, as Douglas Bush points out,[5] a dispenser. Servants' livery, like the insignia and uniform of the Lord Chamberlain's and the King's men, however, also suggests that subjects become iconic versions of the prince, here operating by mirroring abroad the ruler and "dispensing" his or her virtue in their reflection of royalty, or, in fact, specific English royalty, as in the case of the King's men. Such "stewards" are not inferior to, so much as borrowing from, that ruler's official "excellence."

> The summer's flow'r is to the summer sweet,

As the rather surprising metaphoric "answer" to our contemplative "call" begins, the reader enjoys a picture of the beauty of a flower in the context of a whole season—it pleases in every way possible. A flower looks beautiful, smells delightful, but to say that it is sweet suggests taste, a displacement that leads one to include the "rest" of the five senses, touch and hearing. It is fully satisfactory externally to what surrounds it, that is, in my reading, the good ruler in the context of a healthy domain.

> Though to itself it only live and die;

Internally, its life is indifferent to surroundings. It gets no benefit from the splash it makes in the world. Ruling, like being beautiful (summer's flower), only lends one an internal sense of mortality, while it shines eternal to the outer world of "interested" parties who desire its leading attribute.

> But if that flow'r with base infection meet,

As a flower remains vulnerable to interior infection or fungus, and also to external blight, a ruler can forget the good ends of the state and become internally and externally the victim of self-esteem and flattery. "Base" or lowly political infection suggests a ruler's descent into self-interested ambitions, or, even worse, lack of ambition or ideals.

> The basest weed outbraves his dignity:

Wild plants (weeds), by comparison, make the infected flower appear ill. "Weed," as Booth points out, also signifies clothing.[6] Even stewards' stewards "outbrave" the prince's accouterments with their derivative livery, when he or she is morally ill.

> For sweetest things turn sourest by their deeds;

"Sweet" flowers are favored for rule, but that sovereign, by unthinking or ungenerous action, or by inability to act, can become most bitter to the senses and minds of his or her subjects.

> Lilies that fester smell far worse than weeds.

Infected lilies and rulers smell to high heaven, worse than any wild plants, the most lowly citizens, in their corruption. Benevolent deception is an onerous and, possibly, thankless task, but malevolent deception, in Shakespeare's metaphoric argument, actually rusts out, or rather eats out, the soul or innards of the "flower of majesty," leaving only a contemptible rind as remains.

My interpretation of political theory in sonnet 94, if extreme, is not entirely original.[7] In fact, the "new historicists" of the 1980s emphasize the universal "fashioning" of Tudor and Stuart royal images sometimes echoing passages from sonnet 94.[8] But my interpretation obviously suggests Shakespearean belief in a perfectability of benevolent deception that derives from a notion of absolute freedom of invention that followers of Michel Foucault would deny all ages and mind-sets except perhaps our own.

Shakespeare, I argue, suggests an indirect process of rule that is not a mechanism of power, but an organic living out of authority that depends on human genius for its success or failure. Whether or not such radical freedom of thought or action exists in any particular society, I argue that Shakespeare consistently implies that it does. In challenging the concept of ethnic restraint, at least in arguing the consistency of Shakespeare's own theory, I am reviving a notion of the possibility of efficacious benevolent deception, but I do not necessarily espouse it. To test my theory of Shakespeare's view of white Machiavellian politics, I will move on to a picture of its operation in one of Shakespeare's early dramatic portraits of Aristotle's political atom, the family.

2

Teaching the Sly Animal to Be Civil: *The Taming of the Shrew* as Shakespeare's Anatomy of Education

That *The Taming of the Shrew* is a farce[1]—overturning expectations and conservatively resolving them, showing in small and large how "the mechanical encrusted upon the living" can cause laughter to erupt[2]—has gained such currency that a recent critic, Joel Fineman, can conclude that the "play presents" the central eulogies of Kate by Petruchio "as the action of straightforward madness."[3] After all, machinelike playing out of praise paradox is a rhetorical scheme based on a normative impulse. I argue, however, that Petruchio's verbal actions in the play reflect another dramatic conceptualization of the idea of necessary deception, a radical norm, if you will, here in the context of the family-to-be.

In sonnet 94, when Shakespeare says that leaders are "lords and owners of their faces" (1.7), he places himself in a continuum of Renaissance thought about necessary dissembling that dates far into the Middle Ages, even classical times, and yet culminates in Machiavelli's version of the Duke Valentine, Cesare Borgia, the ostensible "hero" of *Il Principe*. Borgia "shows" that he is a right ruler in the social and political body because he can master his "face." He is capable of benevolent deception in a world of fallen men who require deception to curb the civic erosion of egotism and its system of values. For example, Borgia must give the impression of generosity to gain necessary support (chap. 16), but if, in fact, he were generous he would ruin the state by taxation and confiscation. Therefore, he pretends to be generous and fulfills the populace's demand for the appearance of regal liberality. Although he is represented as relatively merciful (chap. 17), Borgia necessarily guards his reputation—in such a fallen age—for cruelty. Thus, according to Machiavelli, the ruler must often appear to be other than he is. He must know how to dissemble or dissimulate or lie for the greater good of the state. In modern terms, a master of the white not the black lie—a kind of constructive hypocrisy—he can perform as a worthy citizen in this waning age of men who lack true Roman *virtù* ("strength of character" or, in fact, "guts") in order to lead them, or simply to get along with them.

Whether or not Shakespeare agrees that the "modern" man is waning—I suspect from a comparison of the Roman plays to the second tetralogy that he does not—he takes a long look at the concept of benevolent deception in several of his plays, early and late. For example, he clearly examines the concept of the Machiavellian "hypocrite" ruler in his picture of the grown-up Hal of *Henry V*, or of *Macbeth*, but the problem of learning how to dissemble and rule through indirection had previously occupied him, not only in the latter three parts of the *Henriad*, but also in his odd picture of education of savagery, *The Taming of the Shrew*.

Since the concept of breeding or instilling humanity in a wild nature is suggested by its very title, I would like to take up this play, for a moment, in its schematic picture of severe grooming. On the negative side, *taming* suggests making civil, politicizing, domesticating, even so-called brainwashing, yet, in a positive light, it can evoke civilizing, bringing up, raising, teaching how to live with and be useful to one's fellows in the *polis*, teaching *realpolitik* and sexual politics as well, and whatever else one normally connects with the word *education*, most notably e-ducation or "leading away out of the savage." Of course, the very term *taming* seems less pejorative in a sixteenth-century pre-Lorentian age where the animal in humankind was generally considered to be a threat to human identity, not one of the essential means of its fulfillment. At any rate, all these concepts of education, pro and con, imply learning to own one's face—that is, dissembling consciously for a higher purpose than self. Candor, for example, in its untamed egoism, violates the social contract. Throughout this play, placed in the elementary political locale of the family or nascent family, Shakespeare seems to be implying that humans must live by certain social rules and work within the political forms of familial life that include (1) apparent recognition of the head of the household and other degrees of rank from spouse to servant, (2) the necessity of controlling moods and speaking up when in doubt, and (3) the need for that very positive kind of hypocrisy, within the hierachical system, that protects people from being brutally candid with one another. Without this ability, humans would be barely human.

The induction to *The Taming of the Shrew* introduces the audience to a savage shrew[4] of a man, unlearned, rude, barbaric, uncivil, perfectly candid, even an endearing beastlike human, offering to punch a woman, probably in the face. Christopher Sly's "I'll pheese[5] you, in faith," that opens the play, is a sworn offer of what in civilized society, with rape and, of course, murder, would constitute the supreme act of barbarity in the realm of social intercourse, a man beating, perhaps altering the precious visage of a woman. As with Caliban and his former attempted rape of Miranda, the audience is immediately alerted to the presence of "he-who-must-be-(or remains to be)-educated-out-of-his-savagery." Civilized society cannot accommodate such behavior. I argue that from this moment Shakespeare will anatomize for us a concept of necessary education in learned hypocrisy, and concomitant self-restraint, in the cases of Sly by the Lord, Grumio by Petruchio, Katherine by Petruchio, Bianca by Katherine, widow by Katherine, and, indeed, Petruchio by Katherine at the very close of the play. All students are sometime savages, instructed in becoming owners of their faces, and so are the members of the audience.

When moviemaker Franco Zeffirelli decided to remove the "Induction" from his cinematic version of Shakespeare's *Taming of the Shrew*, he not only released his film from the strictures of the frame of the stage, its narrow balcony permanently manned by a sleeping Sly, but he also reflected traditional reserve about the presence of that aristocrat of rogues in what otherwise appears to be a healthy romantic comedy. I feel, however, that the action of the Lord instructing Sly the savage in the frame play functions to prepare the audience for the picture of Petruchio instructing Kate and Kate instructing Bianca in the inner play. Like Petruchio, and Katherine in the play's finale, the Lord of the "Induction" appears to be a ruler, tutor and nurturer of some magisterial arrogance, perhaps for cause.

The audience first sees the Lord supervising the care of his prized animals, his hunting dogs, Merriman, Clowder, Silver, Bellman, Echo, an unnamed "deep-mouthed brach" (Ind. 1.16), et al., with the words, "Huntsman, I charge thee, tender well my hounds" (Ind. 1.14). But caring for, raising, training and breeding, "tendering," are all one can hope to do with mere animals. Their bestial souls are not educable in the way of human ones.

Then he comes upon a human animal in paralysis, Christopher Sly, and exclaims: "O monstrous beast, how like a swine he lies!" (Ind. 1.32). Sly enjoys a state that simultaneously combines sleep, drunkenness, and death. To resurrect Sly from the bestial to the human realm, from oblivion to awareness, he must be taught by a "practice" to "forget himself" (Ind. 1.39). He must be taught how to lie about his identity, and ultimately to learn the skill of consciously "owning" his face, the cornerstone of human social intercourse. The Lord employs the reward system for "softening" his subject. He surrounds Sly with soft beds, servants, wanton pictures, music, white wine—all civilized tastes he never acquired—to make him feel alive, well slept, clearheaded—all to get him to say that which is not, that he is truly and honestly a lost lunatic equivalent of the descendant of "Richard Conqueror" he claimed to be in the induction's first scene.

Sly, however, does not begin to crack under this soft-sell "brainwashing" until he is provided with an obedient and announced beauty of a mate, Bartholomew the page in transvestite disguise. Sly alters his behavior only under the pressure to maintain a spurious and impossible marriage. Thus he learns to perform well in society's elementary relationship, in the dance of sexual politics, and, I think, without a soliloquy or an aside, the audience knows Sly does so in a way suggested by his name, in an artful and cunning manner. For only when his wife is introduced as delectable "in this waning age" (Ind. 2.61), does he ask, "Am I a Lord, and have I such a lady?" (Ind. 2.66). Only when that page "in drag" says "I am your wife in all obedience" (Ind. 2.105), does Sly openly lie: "I know it well," followed by "What must I call her?" to give himself the lie. How could he be sure he knew her if he did not know what she was known as?

Bartholomew the page's "wifely obedience," of course, proves to be equally sly when she refuses to "come now to bed," thanks to the hastily concocted lie that "physicians have expressly charged, / In peril to incur your former malady, / That I should yet absent me from your bed" (Ind. 2.119–21). By this time, however, Sly has learned how to be gently hypocritical, if provocative, with the ladies; he has become civilized in his relations with the opposite sex: he complains bawdily, "Ay, it stands so that I may hardly tarry so long—but I would be loath to fall into my dreams again. I will therefore tarry in despite of the flesh and the blood" (Ind. 2.123–25). Then he tentatively settles down in bed to watch a cautionary play on the subject of educating the savage by means of learned hypocrisy, the cohesive element of society. If he had remained awake, he would have learned that if a wife does not pretend to be perfectly loyal and obedient, the husband will run amok, return to the savage rhythm of rape and face-endangering violence. He would have learned that men must acquire the ability to use words as well as violence, although not to immolate all flesh and blood. But Sly has already forgotten his old bestial self by learning to own his face.

Petruchio, in the play within a play, most clearly owns his face, for example, with his claim of purely mercenary ends to his mating, belied by his painstaking training of Katherine, or by his systematic provocation of all Paduans by means of irony and sarcasm. The soft-sell "brainwashing" of Sly by the Lord parallels the hard-sell "brainwashing" of Katherine by Petruchio. She must learn to pretend perfect obedience and loyalty in civilized hypocrisy through a system of hazing that reaches its goal precisely when she learns to "say that which is not" out of apparent obedience to her husband, that is, when she overcomes her tendency to brutal candor:

> *Hortensio.* [*Aside to Kate.*] Say as he says or we shall never go.
> *Kate.* Forward, I pray, since we have come so far,
>   And be it moon or sun or what you please.
>   An if you please to call it a rush-candle,
>   Henceforth I vow it shall be so for me.
> *Petruchio.* I say it is the moon.
> *Kate.*   I know it is the moon.
> *Petruchio.* Nay, then you lie. It is the blessèd sun.
> *Kate.* Then God be blessed, it is the blessèd sun,
>   But sun it is not when you say it is not,
>   And the moon changes even as your mind.
>
>   (4.5.11–20)

When Kate injects her final remark, we see she is free to criticize her husband—indeed gently to call him a lunatic—so long as she plays by the rules of apparent obedience and the white lies she has learned to live by. Of course, she must learn exactly the extent the mind of her otherwise amiable Petruchio is moonlike or changeable, and when his fit is upon him she will have to control his very male "berserker" lunacy with the tact that he had the presence of mind to teach her. Without the social adhesion of not entirely candid owning of one's face, family can degenerate into a state of beastly violence or into a kind of stasis that is equally savage and unregenerative. This concept of educable static savagery helps explain, I think, the importance to Sly's cautionary play of the sometimes ignored Lucentio-Bianca plot.[6]

"Baptista Minola of *Padua, father of Kate and Bianca*," lives in a botched family, a family that has returned to a state of savagery, leveled out by a peculiar disorder in rule. Order apparently disappeared when the father came to favor his younger daughter, Bianca, over his older daughter, Kate. Kate names her father the cause of disorder when she says of Minola's regard for Bianca, "She is your treasure" (2.1.32). Minola's apparently impossible demand that Katherine be married first has become, in fact, a means of keeping "precious" Bianca at home. The two sisters "go savage" in the two classic ways—Kate, actively, Bianca, passively. Kate pictures forth active or violent savagery, like Sly's, not only in tying her sister's hands in order to beat her, breaking the lute over Hortensio's head, and striking Petruchio, but also in verbal violence directed at Petruchio and others. She can, if necessary, assault with the best words. For example, restrained from physical violence, she can call her future husband both insane and cowardly with rapier-like wit. He is "one half lunatic, / A madcap ruffian and a swearing Jack, / That thinks with oaths to face the matter out" (2.1.289–91). But her "wild-Kate's" violence is matched by the obverse side of savagery in Bianca, its antinomy. The younger sister uses the silent treatment, and all savage "cats" know this form of barbarity as well.

When Kate is asked to explain her violent behavior toward her sister, who never crossed her "with a bitter word" (2.1.28), she says "Her silence flouts me and I'll be revenged." Indeed the manipulation of humans by glaring and moping—by failing to use the resources of language to make one's fellows feel well with the world—is, according to Shakespeare's apparent schematization, a scourge that "flouts," that stings with as much savagery as the "physical" and the "verbal" whip. And Shakespeare has constructed his plot to expose this very duality. When Kate comes around to instructing her sister in constructive hypocrisy at the play's close, she dwells on Bianca's "guilt-tripping" version of savagery in all its own barbaric lunacy:

> Fie, fie, unknit that threat'ning unkind brow
> And dart not scornful glances from those eyes
> To wound thy lord, thy king, thy governor.
> It blots thy beauty as frosts do bite the meads,
> Confounds thy fame as whirlwinds shake fair buds,
> And in no sense is meet or amiable.

> A woman moved is like a fountain troubled,
> Muddy, ill-seeming, thick, bereft of beauty,
> And while it is so, none so dry or thirsty
> Will deign to sip or touch one drop of it.
>
> (5.2.141–50)

Katherine's picture of a beautiful woman as man's sustenance, the cure for thirst, suggests not only man's joy in her beauty and compliance but in those beautiful words which are being replaced in Bianca's behavior by mute voice and scornful glance. Kate emphasizes the savagery of the silent treatment by the violence implicit in her metaphors of "darting" and "wounding,"[1] and the self-violence implicit in "blotting," "biting," and "shaking." Of course Katherine has learned how to reach her self-consciously beautiful sister by means of the indirection of tact. Love poets have always known that scornful looks can be erotic, but to move her sister she will argue that such glances erode her image. They make her clear water "muddy" and "thick." When, at the end of her great men-pleasing speech, when she calls her sister and the widow "froward and unable worms" (5.2.174), Katherine still reminds them of the means of savage guilt-tripping, hurt silence. If they owned their faces, they would never allow their moods to metamorphose them into such beasts, and unawares. Worms or dragons, they are behaving like members of the mythical animal, not the human, kingdom.

Critics have noted that in sleeping through his cautionary play, Sly could not have gotten its message.[7] But as I have suggested, I believe he showed he understood its point when he learned to lie about knowing his page-wife. What has he learned? That all people must bend somewhat to fit the shape of others, by indirection, by self-control. Shakespeare does not employ the metaphor of hypocrisy and the white lie as social cohesive or glue. His leading image comes from a technicality of sixteenth-century bowling: the bias.[8] When Katherine finally admits that she is willing to say the sun is the moon and vice versa according to Petruchio's wish, he responds

> Thus the bowl should run
> And not unluckily against the bias.
>
> (4.5.24–25)

Here I hold he argues that Kate, with her candid, savage, naturally selfish ways, was like a ball in lawn bowls unable to close in on life's happy goal (the jack) because she struggled (went straight) "unluckily" against the bias of society itself and rolled out of bounds. That society should require an unstraight or curving thing, conformable to a spin caused by the insertion of a lead weight on one side of a ball (to create a lopsided effect), also suggests the necessary deviousness that allows humans to live with humans like humans not like beasts (be they wildcats, worms, dragons, or swine).

Opponents of the Renaissance school of necessary lying did not merely reside behind cloistered walls. Montaigne noted that corrosive effect of lying on the soul by way of internal "bleeding" created by the speaking conscience. Shakespeare himself took up Montaigne, later, in the obverse of the sunny mood seen here, to look into the unspeakable unhappiness and self-destruction of dissemblers such as Iago and Macbeth. In fact, the notion of dissembling clowns and jesters on the English stage darkens considerably between the time of Feste and that of Bosola. Perhaps the most memorable argument for society's need for indirection and hypocrisy is contained in Erasmus's *Encomium Moriae* at the opening of the English Renaissance inside the Court of Henry VIII. And the most powerful argument against falsehood of any sort is contained in Milton's lonely picture of Satan after the close of the Interregnum. Shakespeare did not take a middle road on the issue. Sometimes pro, sometimes con, he took radical views of lying, in *The Taming of the Shrew*, as essential to the education of the savage.

When I examine Macbeth's grotesque imagination in chapter 10, the festering lily of deception becomes internally a "bloody" horror. But in Shakespeare's "sunshine" comedy, *Taming of the Shrew*, all deception is white, not black, and as symbolized by the bias in lawn bowls, it only facilitates appropinquity among potential savages of the active and passive persuasion. Social order, Shakespeare "argues," requires such appropinquation. Since comedy ritualizes joining, nearness, and marriage, it necessarily sacralizes the crooked means of approaching the ball to the jack, the bias of benevolent deception being its method. In the later history plays, Shakespeare will show the strains of would-be benevolent deception in the character of the ruler. And then in the tragedies he will show how it can utterly isolate the individual. Therefore, I now move on to Hal's sometimes darker thoughts on the effect or princes not doing "the thing they most do show."

3

From Hal to Henry V: The Deceptive Ruler and His Discontents

In his early argument in favor of a dialectical and "ambivalent" Shakespeare, as I have noted, A. P. Rossiter invokes sonnet 94 to ask if inevitable forces of separation make Prince Hal, "the actor in public affairs assume a predetermined part, like a *play*-actor only with all of his directives outside and none of his? One of those 'who, moving others, are themselves as stone,' as the sonnet phrases it: 'the lords and owners of their faces'?"[1] Obviously for Rossiter these lines from sonnet 94 represent a necessary evil. Thus he deemphasizes the cardinal "But if" at the opening of line 11 that I have just depended on to hinge my argument. Rossiter, however, also suggests a deterministic—if ambiguous—historical setting for Hal's and Henry's action that I do not see borne out by Shakespeare's figure of the Henry Monmouth in the final three plays of the second tetralogy. In my reading, Shakespeare presents a Hal consciously and consistently manipulating his image both in play and in ceremonial office for the very "moral" purpose of benefiting the state and his own and his friends' well-being. He deceives happily when he is at play, more sadly when he is weighted down with fashioning his own "majesty" for specific political purposes, but in all cases, Shakespeare exposes both Hal's theoretical bias—which I argue does not change—and his freedom of choice and self-mastery, perhaps most emphatically in Henry's two extended internal monologues.

At the very close of act 1, scene 2 of 1 *Henry IV* (ll 183–205),and near the end of act 4, scene 1 of *Henry V* (ll. 216–70), Shakespeare offers two widely separated chances to look into the political thought of Shakespeare's and, I believe, Britain's most striking literary version of the epic hero,[2] once as a seeming prodigal madcap Prince of Wales and once as a solemn ruler on a purportedly sanctified mission to conquer France, a king who, disguised as a combatant named Harry le Roy has just inspected, in defilade, his own army. Of course, my very epithets, "seeming," "purportedly," "disguised," and "in defilade" load my argument in favor of an image of deception in this prince, but, in fact, Hal's two well-organized tone-poems-as-soliloquies-on-politics openly develop our hero's own concept of the necessary "hypocrisy" of rule.

Shakespeare links these two extended soliloquies by keying them on the notion of the gap or distance between effective political show and the actual inner feelings of its creator. In the former case, Hal presents a positive history of present and future deception in the development of "charisma" in light of man's need for contrariety. In the latter, King Henry exposes the onerous aspect of continually sacrificing himself in order to produce, for the good of the land, a ceremonial self-image. This image of state, his "public body," he argues, merely ensures that the subjects of the realm will be able to target the iconic "king" for irrational or justifiable blame, for flattery and adulation, while his private body goes sleepless.

That one soliloquy seems light, even, to some post-romantic readers, a little smug,[3] and the other somber and self-searching, does not, I argue, reflect in some simple way Henry's development from boy to man, or from rebel subject to ruler. The contexts differ radically. Hal's early speech is lightened by his "pastoral" joy in his friends and the anticipation of Poins's classic practical joke on Falstaff. The second, in the necessarily dictatorial context of combat, is darkened by discovery of an assassination plot directed at him as well as trepidation on the eve of the Battle of Agincourt. Actually, the two soliloquies present variations on a theme similar to those found in the "call" and "answer" of sonnet 94. Externally, godlike manipulation of the body politic can be happy, but internally the "flower" or "lily" of princedom suffers the most ordinary diseases and "dis-eases." Thus, I argue that the two speeches demonstrate little or no change in Henry Monmouth's political philosophy, merely a difference in mood resulting from his vastly diverse circumstances.

When the Prince of Wales opens his early soliloquy with "I know you all, and will awhile upold / The unyoked humor of your idleness," the audience understands—somewhat jarringly—that Hal is not only not that profligate roisterer just beheld on the stage, but that with consummate control he has been juggling his image for an ulterior motive. Warnings that his image will change from apparent wastrel to one of authority when he becomes king, however, have just informed all his verbal duels with Falstaff, who, "melancholy as a gib-cat or a lugged bear" (1.2.68), asks him if he will condemn thieves of the night when he ascends the throne: "Shall there be gallows standing in England when thou art king" (1.2.54)? To this his friend delivers an implicit affirmative. By means of internal monologue, Hal now lets it be known that both his first and second self-images, wastrel and king, are elements of a precise political scheme to create white magical charm in him that may be used to save England from civil war and lesser forms of internal dissension. Hal will vastly increase the impact of his career on the public by pretending both profligacy and reformation from profligacy. Thus, echoing the parable of the prodigal son, he develops the central image of the sun (which also suggests sun-king, and, by wordplay, "son," the son of a king) to show why the perversity of the human political animal requires such deception. Because "nothing pleaseth [humans] but rare accidents" (1.2.195), he will fabricate one in his own demeanor. As the English sun so often remains on the far side of the "base contagious clouds" (1.2.186), in order to be longed for, so will Hal enjoy unequaled love when he seems to experience a "reformation." Had Hal been consistently "good," he could neither "falsify men's hopes" for his downfall, nor surprise them with his brilliance.

Thus Hal says that a king must remember that unalloyed truth will have no "glitter" for a fickle populace. It must be "grounded," in this case, in a false image of former corruption. To this purpose, Hal employs the metaphor of a setting for his metal (which also implies his "mettle" or true worth):

> like bright metal on a sullen ground,
> My reformation, glitt'ring o'er my fault,
> Shall show more goodly and attract more eyes
> Than that which hath no foil to set it off.
>
> (1.2.200–203)

By marvelous contrariety, men only truly prize what they do not have, and in reversing their expectations of him, Hal can expect to control the unruly lands his father could not. To mark the end of the scene, Hal triumphantly delivers a couplet on his manipulation of outward seeming:

> I'll so offend to make offense a skill,
> Redeeming time when men think least I will.

Men will not merely think; they will hope. But his reversal of their hopes may preserve England as a nation and Great Britain as an empire.

M. M. Reese, in his powerful investigation of the nature of *Henry V* as a compendium of Shakespearean ideals of majesty, suggests that "Henry's speech on ceremony" (4.1.216–70) is a reversion to Hal's thoughts "back in the taverns"[4] and, in the context of an epical *Henry V*, it provides "a moment of weakness." I argue, however, that the high seriousness of Hal's political ideas in his soliloquy in Eastcheap is restated and amplified in this, his most extensive interior monologue. The very extent of this self-examination reflects a context that leads to Henry's internalization of anger and sorrow at his necessary image-making. Again the populace behaves in a perverse manner, here burdening the ruler with its own moral and spiritual discomfort. As Henry proceeds to develop a notion of the internal damage resulting from the load of a ceremonial regal self-image that attracts all public blame, he says that we, the citizens, "and our sins, lay on the king! / We must bear all" (218–9). In Henry's melancholic and self-obsessed statement, the "we" of the populace immediately shifts to the "we" of fellow rulers burdened by the commonwealth or, in fact, something akin to the "papal we" of England's king. The iconic load that Hal took up so lightly in his projected "reformation" weighs heavily at this moment, as if he now becomes the bearer of general sins, a scapegoat branded for denigration in his army, ultimately, perhaps, for assassination.

Again he invokes the concept of the internal and external body of the king as targets of public attention. Thus is he "Twin-born with greatness, subject to the breath / Of every fool, whose sense no more can feel / But his own wringing" (219–22). He becomes identified with public suffering, the recipient of "wringing" (222), "mortal griefs" (228), "fearing" (235), the "suffering" of the "wretched slave" (254), and the "distress" of "distressful bread" (256), that all lead to private insomnia. Hollow "Ceremony" proves a vast receptacle of public distress.

Somewhat in the vein of Falstaff's attacks on the concept of "honor" in *1 Henry IV* (5.1.27ff. and 5.3.55ff.), Henry asks rhetorically how Ceremony can cure him of damages from the twin poison of flattery and blame. Thus he rues the artificiality of place necessary to rule men, a hollow sacrificial "god . . . that suffer'st more / Of mortal griefs than do thy worshippers" (227). Henry asks of this "idol Ceremony" (226):

> Art thou aught else but place, degree, and form,
> Creating awe and fear in other men?
>
> (232–33)

"Ceremony" keeps men orderly in the realm by example of "place, degree, and form," while his actual inner self suffers sleepless "horrid night" (257). Thus his central image becomes the absence of insomnia among the lowest rank in the kingdom, the slave, who "all night / Sleeps in Elysium" (259–60). All this regal ceremony becomes on his part a mere disadvantaged game of tennis, where the kingdom's lowest ranked citizen has "the forehand and vantage of a king" (266).

If, in his darkest moment, Henry V pictures himself as a human sacrifice to monarchic care and public "dis-ease," he is directly reflecting the thought that Hal early developed concerning benevolent deception of rulers. Therefore, I argue, rather than displaying development of thinking on power, these two soliloquies represent the two aspects, external and internal, of the necessary artificiality of rule. *Allegro*, Hal praises the supreme joy of image-making of the lily; *penseroso*, he tells only of its internal discontents that could easily lead to "festering" and self-victimization. Henry Monmouth's joy will, in fact, return in his gamelike, humor-filled manipulation of "fair Katherine" (5.2.98,104). But in both rare cases of extended internal monologue, what is seen is a consistent understanding of the separation of image-making and the internal joy or distress in its making and effects. In one arena, position mandates control; in the other, it requires the churning of inward aggression or discontent that, in Macbeth's case, as I shall note in chapter 10, can murder sleep.

Since I have concentrated on Shakespeare's image of the ruler and his distress, let me now turn to his picture of disease and "dis-ease" among the "ruled," whether they be aristocrat or peasant, lieutenant or soldier. Here I will demonstrate that Shakespeare expresses political theory so consistently, through his characters, that his very choice of images reflects a theory of "non-rule," and becomes as much his "signature" as his autograph itself. Again, when I examine one culmination of his picture of "leveling," in *Julius Caesar*, it will be shown that his play is schematized according to this negative picture of the human political animal.

PART 2
Leveling, through Rivalry and Victimization

4

"Remorse in Myself with His Words": Shakespeare's Schematic Picture of Factional Behavior

Thanks in part to the publication of Sir Thomas More in 1844 and the discovery that three pages of the original manuscript of its "Ill May Day Scene," its picture of civil disturbance in London, were in Shakespeare's hand, readers in the last century and a half have combed all Shakespeare's scenes of political unrest for traces of political bias, theory, or, indeed, confusion.[1] Jack Cade's rebellion in 2 Henry VI, the crowd scenes in Shakespeare's Rome of Julius Caesar and Coriolanus, and Ulysses' analysis of political troubles in the Greek council scene of Troilus and Cressida provide central locations.

"Old historical" investigations of Shakespeare's politics have discovered Shakespeare's probable political stance in terms of such modern formulations as "radical, liberal, conservative," and so forth. Such interpreters tend to ask "Does Shakespeare want us to sympathize with individual citizens under Cade's or Anthony's or Lincoln's or the Tribunes' influence?" "Does Shakespeare accept deposition as a rightful form of political turnover? In all cases? In some cases? Only in Roman cases? In no cases?" On the whole, they conclude with R. W. Chambers that

> It is not so easy to refute the American democrat when, amid much that is exaggerated and absurd, he writes "There can easily be too much liberty according to Shakespeare, but the idea of too much authority is foreign to him."[2]

Chambers argues that for the sake of a macrocosmic and microcosmic idea of stability and peace, Shakespeare brooked little or no "insubordination," and some recent critics have followed this line. Speaking of Jack Cade's rebellion, David Bevington says that, thanks to conservative political bias, "Shakespeare's use of chronicles indicates his unsparing denunciation" of Cade's insurrection. "His ridicule of Utopian communism, and his ascription to Cade of stupidity and clumsiness, are invented."[3] Of course, the biographical Shakespeare was hardly immobile in the social structure of England. And it may seem odd that the supposed hater of insubordination moved up two or three classes in his day, from actor/author to entrepreneur to gentleman/landowner. However, that self-made men are tempted to become authoritarian is axiomatic. The attempt to locate the supposed ideology of this Renaissance playwright in the terms of twentieth-century political grids, with their uncertain lefts and rights, invites the use of what is known of his biography for support.

In "new historical" circles, Shakespeare is rarely allowed the freedom of emotion or intellect that could produce consistent bias or theory concerning so crucial a topic as civil disturbance. Greenblatt, Dollimore, and other theorists claim that cultural pressure produced an adherence and resistance to positions of power that make of Shakespeare's text a map of authoritarian control and rebellion. For example, in the case of Shakespeare's purportedly chaotic picture of civil disturbance in *Troilus and Cressida*, Dollimore challenges Richard Fly's argument[4] that Shakespeare consciously presents "disjunction" to symbolize disorder, and says that "to the extent that it posits an underlying, primordial state of dislocation, the language of chaos [Ulysses' speech on degree, for example] mystifies social process,"[5] a process Dollimore demystifies according to the macrocosm of the dialectic of history and exploded theory. But what happens if one looks for consistency in Ulysses' speech and tries to demystify its apparently disparate images *in se*? Suddenly a different and, I think, more ominous, picture of leveling makes its appearance.

A curious by-product of investigation of Shakespeare's versions of civil disturbance has been the location of what William Matchett—borrowing a term from Edward A. Armstrong's *Shakespeare's Imagination*—called a "thought or image cluster," an idiosyncratic set of thoughts, images, and words that Shakespeare returns to when he presents political unrest, in the case in question—Matchett's summary of Chambers's findings—a sequence of

> five elements—rebellion against (or neglect of) degree, a river in flood, the aged or the very young as victims, cannibal monsters, and using knees as feet.[6]

Readers, according to Matchett, could invoke such a cluster to act as a kind of mental signature of Shakespeare and use it to help determine the authorship of a passage from a doubtfully Shakespearean scene or play such as "The Ill May Day Scene" of *Sir Thomas More*. I would like to take a close look at the "image cluster," as Matchett calls it—developed first by Chambers on two occasions, and by Karl P. Wentersdorf[7] on one—in order to suggest a Shakespearean schematization of factional behavior. I argue that rather than favoring and theatrically promoting a single political faction or even political bias, Shakespeare develops a notion of an aspect of human nature, as he apparently sees it, presented in a group of linking poetic images on diverse occasions. Patrician or plebeian, or somewhere in between, humans always risk losing a sense of their own individual characters, their difference, if you will, in crowds, groups, and factions. They may revert to leveling, where they would annihilate all distinctions, even those made by words. But poetic—that is, the most "distinctive"—words can save them, and, in *Sir Thomas More* and *Coriolanus*, they do.

According to Chambers's cluster, the leader of the collective forces of citizens in all four of our crowd scenes, first of all, calls for "rebellion against (or neglect of) degree." This resistance to "place" is also, ostensibly, the subject of Ulysses' speech to the Greek council, and thus, it can be "aristocratic." But its mention by an agitator in a rebellious group is taken to be transparent by some of Shakespeare's best readers. Supposedly, Chambers argues, absence of degree allows one to choose at random a higher place for oneself. Insubordinate men want good fortune thrust upon them, though perhaps they do not deserve it. The group of commoners want to be aristocrats or, for that matter, monarchs all. As Clifford suggests, Cade would make the "meanest of you earls and dukes" (*2 Henry VI* 4.8.35). In the *More* fragment all would "sytt as kings."[8] And yet in *Julius Caesar*, the *More* fragment, and *Coriolanus*, such aspiring commoners are consistently referred to as less than human, thus actually deserving of no place at all. In *Julius Caesar*, for example, the tribune Marullus calls the plebeians "You blocks, you stones, you worse than senseless things" (1.1.35). London Sheriff Thomas More calls the crowd congregated for civil disturbance "poor things," with the emphasis, I think, on the latter word. In one series of speeches, Marcius refers to the plebians in rebellion as "curs" (1.1.163), "hares," "foxes," "geese," "quartered slaves" (194), and finally "fragments." And when Ulysses says that neglect of degree will create "an universal wolf" (1.3.121), it might be easy to conclude with Chambers that the problem is simply one of Shakespeare's apprehension of insubordination among the patently undeserving, the bestial and insensitive lower orders.

An examination of the context of these scenes, however, suggests that apparent loss of a sense of identity of these guildsmen and other factions is matched by a loss of identity among the so-called "ruling classes" and that the problem of loss of degree is "universal." In fact, what scrambling exists among the crowds in city streets also appears in various courts. If the commoners must rule in a disorderly fashion, their "superiors" refuse to rule in an orderly fashion. If one says "insubordination" in one case, one might say "insuperioration" in the other. Human nature in confusion about personal "character" in society seems to be Shakespeare's true subject. Therefore, Ulysses' remarks about subhuman behavior refer strictly to the actions of aristocratic if not heroic or semidivine Greeks. On the whole, the plays present a "general" breakdown of identity in a specific case—even among such "generals" as Agamemnon, Achilles, and Ajax—a case where all humans are behaving in a uniformly erratic fashion, unstayed by any sense of personal "character" or "difference."

Although it does not appear in Chambers's cluster, the "image" that perhaps best suggests the "thought" that Shakespeare seems to reiterate in his scenes of unrest is that of "uniform or similar clothing," one that does not suggest upward mobility so much as leveling. Jack Cade "the clothier means to dress the commonwealth" (4.2.4–5) in common colors. He says he "will apparel them all in one livery, that they may agree like brothers and worship me their lord" (4.2.67–69). Here each "working" person's identity will be lost in one idolatrous incorporate "self-agreeable" individual. But such loss of a sense of one's rank or position in society in *2 Henry VI* is not restricted to the butchers and clothiers, but includes the King and his court. As Bevington has pointed out, Cade's rebellion is "symptomatic of social disorder"[9] that begins with "lack of leadership in the ruling class."[10] The identity of the "king" as "ruling" or "leader" is lost in Henry's pastoral quest for the livery of a saint. The school of cardinals should "set the triple crown upon his head" (1.3.61)— that of a pope—not the double one of France and England. He too confuses his accouterments and garments.

Julius Caesar opens with much ado on the tribunes' part about the tradesmen's "best apparel" (1.1.8), that apparently disguises their identity as specific guildsmen. Flavius says, "you ought not walk / Upon a laboring day without the sign / Of your profession." The impertinent cobbler and others have worn indistinguishable "holiday" attire rather than the various "livery" of "mechanical" (1.1.3) people, tradesmen. Here the tribunes sense the danger of collective violence in the lower orders. But the aristocratic conspiracy against Caesar also wears a curious uniform. When the conspirators appear at night, Lucius cannot distinguish them. He says that he can, "by no means," "discover them / By any mark of favor" (2.1.75–76). Brutus, worrying about this uniform "dis-guise," observes in monologue that this "faction" can hardly hope to "mask" its "monstrous visage" by day. The group that he joins thus becomes for Brutus a "monster" clothed in one identifiable and willful opinion. As More says with, I think, characteristic Shakespearean punning to the Ill May Day crowd, "You in ruff of your opynions clothd" (211) are indistinguishable from other "ruffians . . . with sealf same hand sealf reasons and sealf right" (212). Identical "ruffs" (collars) make for "ruffians" (rowdies, brutes), ready, perhaps, for "rough" practice. In *Coriolanus*, the "leveling" of clothing is evoked as the citizens puzzle about the "diversely colored" (2.3.18ff.) wits of the "many-headed multitude" at the moment when Coriolanus appears "in a gown of humility." And Ulysses remarks in *Troilus and Cressida* that "degree being vizarded, / Th'unworthiest shows as fairly in the mask" (1.3.83). The mask ("facial disguise") suggests metaphoric sameness, as opposed to distinguishable character, suitable to a mask ("costume party") or masque ("court entertainment") where distinction between "characters" and their inner identity is lost.

I feel that Shakespeare does not express an antipathy to holding things in common or of the "utopian" collective ideal in this emphasis on loss of a personal sense of identity—or difference—in a crowd. Shakespeare can share in the praise of life away from hierarchy, for example, in the magical songs of *As You Like It*, such as "Under the Greenwood Tree." Cooperation in Shakespeare remains, perhaps, the highest political ideal. Here, however, there is a comment on group behavior in cases of panic or uncontrolled revelry, the realm of Dionysus. When people all join in common action, they suspend their sense of self, their self-will, their self-thought. Distinction is gone. This identity-less "state" has an active side and a passive one. One aspect is violent, focused on victims blamed for the disorder itself. The passive side, however, as I hope will be clearer when I touch on

Chamber's final image of "knees as feet," is religious. People collectively dissolve "selfness" both in violence and in ritual, and the two "holiday" states are closely, dangerously, connected in Shakespeare's plays, apparently by design.

In the context of group action, the four actual images of the cluster of thoughts and representations following "rebellion against (or neglect of) degree" suddenly fit together in a familiar way. First of all, the flood breaking its bounds, whether of riverbank—"a river in flood"—or seashore, now suggests the uncontrolled power and mobility of urban crowd behavior that takes all with it, like other natural disasters such as fire, earthquake, and plague. Images of these other catastrophes lie close to flood images in these five plays, fire in 2 Henry VI, plague and unnamed infection in Sir Thomas More, storms and plagues in Julius Caesar, "contagion" and "boils and plagues" (1.4.30) in Coriolanus. When Ulysses speaks of floods, he couples such natural disaster with the breakup of the cosmos.

> But when the planets
> In evil mixture to disorder wander,
> What plagues, and what portents, what mutiny,
> What raging of the sea, shaking of earth,
> Commotion in the winds, frights, changes, horrors,
> Divert and crack, rend and deracinate
> The unity and married calm of states
> Quite from their fixture?
>
> (1.3.94–101)

Obviously, "plague" becomes as central an image as flood for factional behavior, perhaps because it is a human affliction and because it is "catching" like the "envious fever / Of pale and bloodless emulation" (1.3.133–34) that Ulysses emphasizes at the close of his speech. Ulysses suggests that envy and emulation[11] are the first steps toward suspension of one's individuality that eventually lead to participation in uniformly motivated action. In all Shakespeare's scenes of civil disturbance, men and women fearfully vie with each other and lose themselves in "emulation" of what they thought they opposed.

When civil order finally breaks down—when there are no policemen, so to speak—"the aged or the very young"—our second image in the "cluster"—inevitably become "victims" thanks to their relative vulnerability. A new savage principle—the rule of force—is invoked, and only the strongest survive. In Antony's words

> mothers shall but smile when they behold
> Their infants quarter èd with the hands of war,
> All pity choked with custom of fell deeds.
>
> (3.1.267–69)

Perhaps because women—with the exception of Amazons—are—with military hardware—the most prized "possessions" in a world ruled by brute force, they are less vulnerable than the "old and very young," and thus they chance to live on to observe the destruction of the less protected members of their families.

In our third image, the member of the collective force becomes a "cannibal monster" because he eats up other humans, eats up his own family, and finally himself: that is, he ultimately cannibalizes self. Ulysses says,

> Then everything include itself in power,
> Power into will, will into appetite.
> And appetite, an universal wolf,
> So doubly seconded with will and power,
> Must make perforce an universal prey
> And last eat up himself.
>
> (1.3.119–24)

That Ulysses mentions "great Agamemnon" at this moment suggests the possibility that the disorder in the Greek camp was set in motion by the commander in chief's unmentionable—and unmentioned—squabble over Briseis and the other spoils with his "lieutenant" Achilles. The scramble that follows such envious emulation will, if it is not stayed, cause all faction in the Greek camp ultimately to eat up itself.

The fourth image of "knees as feet," finally, seems at first to suggest the posture of begging for mercy from a "higher power." But in Shakespeare's scenes, such higher power rarely makes its appearance. The world has been leveled. The image of knees as feet, I feel, suggests ritual observance of unanimity of will. Violent factional behavior in Shakespeare always seeks two forms of self-justification. In one case it "reasons" that when it is destroying an individual, it is performing ritual sacrifice in order to appease the gods. Here holiday gear and using knees as feet are appropriate. As justification for killing Caesar, Brutus says

> Let's be sacrificers, but not butchers, Caius . . .
> Let's kill him boldly, but not wrathfully;
> Let's carve him as a dish fit for the gods.
>
> (2.1.166, 172–73)

Brutus's hypnotic anaphora disguises a chilling misuse of ritual, recalling 1 Rebel's justification of slaughter in *2 Henry VI*:

> Then is sin struck down like an ox and iniquity's throat cut like a calf. (4.2.24–25)

The suggestion of ritual sacrifice, however, is not entire pretense. An attempt to end all strife by means of unanimous presence at sacrifice remains possible, as long as the victim remains a "universal" symbol.

A second means of justification, the faction's system of justice, however, is a travesty of court systems, designed to squelch all "trial," all debate, in fact, all words. In *2 Henry VI*, a so-called fair trial of the Clerk of Chartham is staged when Cade claims he is "sorry" (4.2.85) to hear the clerk can "make obligations and write courthand," but Cade says,

> The man is a proper man, of mine honor. Unless I find him guilty, he shall not die. Come hither, sirrah, I must examine thee. What is thy name?
> *Clerk.* Emmanuel.
> *Butcher.* They use to write it on the top of letters. 'Twill go hard with you.
> *Cade.* Let me alone. Dost thou use to write thy name? or hast thou a mark to thyself, like an honest plain-dealing man?
> *Clerk.* Sir, I thank God, I have been so well brought up that I can write my name.
> *All.* He hath confessed. Away with him! He's a villain and a traitor.
> *Cade.* Away with him, I say. Hang him with his pen and inkhorn about his neck. (4.2.85–98)

No doubt Bevington would take this interrogation to be an example of Shakespeare's unauthorized yet orthodox "ascription to Cade of 'stupidity,'"[12] but I think Shakespeare also has a schematic motive that exposes a perfectly "rational" argument. In this ludicrous examination, ability with the written word and the mention of God seem to doom the clerk in arbitrary fashion, because words imply distinctions and the mention of a word for God, "Emmanuel," for example, may be used to contain violence in ritual thanksgiving. Like the staged pleading for Publius Cimber of the senatorial conspirators and the arbitrary questioning of Cinna the poet in *Julius Caesar*, as shall be seen in chapter 5, there is here a case of judicial parody, a mere ruse used to facilitate surrounding the victim. In all cases, dismemberment of the victim follows. Finally, in *Coriolanus* the citizens reach an utterly arbitrary "verdict" (1.1.10) that Marcius is helping Rome only out of pride and regard for his mother. Clearly, in such a breakdown, as Ulysses says in *Troilus and Cressida*, "Force should be . . . justice, too" (1.3.116). The legal system designed to protect the old and very young from brute strength is cynically travestied by a judicial apparatus that automatically justifies its own force.

In *2 Henry VI*, the first victim is William, the Clerk of Chartham, who can ("O monstrous") "write and read and cast accompt" (4.2.77). In *Julius Caesar*, when Cinna establishes his identity as a poet and not a conspirator, the audience hears that he is to be torn "for his bad verses" (3.3.30). Here one is reminded that the playwright himself—and his "bad" verse—may be the target of collective violence. Shakespeare has again reminded us of his tenuous relationship with his audience and his "readers." Jack Cade best describes the reaction of the faction to effective "poetic" language when he speaks of the emotional force of Lord Say's speech at the moment the Lord is to be carried off and beheaded with his son:

> I feel remorse in myself with his words, but I'll bridle it. He shall die, an it be but for pleading so well for his life. (4.7.97–99)

Such remorse did not delay ("bridle") but hastened Cade's destruction of Lord Say. He used ("bridled") the energy pity infused in him for the purpose of violence.

In all these cases of justification of group murder, one is reminded that the victim is a man of words. That system of distinctions, language, the giver of civility, apparently must be obliterated with its speaker. Casca, who first stabs Caesar, apparently angry with Caesar's words, says "Speak hands for me" (3.1.76), as if reducing language once and for all to hands and the arms they hold. In *Coriolanus* "all" want "no more talking on't" (1.1.11). The citizens determine to tear apart Marcius—a man of many inflammatory words—but Menenius Agrippa's poetic fable comes between them and their common wish.

Order in Rome is magically reestablished by Menenius's words. In the delivery of the fable of the stomach and the parts, as with Sir Thomas More's speech in the "Ill May Day Scene," words can suddenly appease a crowd. Now the reiterate flood image is applied not to the undifferentiated energy of the crowd but to the growth of the Roman Empire, a flood that will defeat their flood, as fire checks fire. Menenius asks the citizens slyly to imagine their flood coming in conflict with

> the Roman state, whose course will on
> The way it takes, cracking ten thousand curbs
> Of more strong link asunder than can ever
> Appear in your impediment.
>
> (1.1.65–68)

As Sir Philip Sidney demonstrated in his *Defence of Poetry*,[13] Menenius Agrippa becomes a consummate artist—like Nathan with David—at tapping an undifferentiated audience with words of distinction. Here Menenius's poetic words stymie the crowd who are seeking to cut off all words at their source.

Poets in the age of Elizabethan monarchic rule, like the Augustan poets, were, of course, in one sense, political writers supporting the regime and its aims. Occasionally, brighter stars, regally adopted ones, like Sidney, Spenser, and Shakespeare, were allowed to make what seem to be "underground" and specific comments in the mode of "coterie" animadversion on the queen's policies, such as her creation of personal favorites and public alliances, but espousing generalized political doctrine to the right or left of Elizabeth would be impossible to publish, or punishable if it were, especially on the stage.[14] The censors and other authorities would excise. Though I feel that one can only guess Shakespeare's own personal bias, he often analyzes man the political animal in his own apparent universal terms. As a factional creature, humans are pictured as not only incapable of reason, but as would-be obliterators of same. They would destroy the medium of discourse and of poetry, meaningful words. In the best of cases, however, poetic words and their distinctions can suddenly prove their savior. In some of Shakespeare's tragedies, however, such as *Julius Caesar* or *Macbeth*, such a redemptive process, though it remains implied, never emerges, as I will show in chapter 5.

5
"The Teeth of Emulation": Failed Sacrifice in Shakespeare's *Julius Caesar*

Brents Stirling, in his seminal essay on reference to primitive sacrificial customs in *Julius Caesar*, " 'Or Else This Were a Savage Spectacle,' " argues that ritual terminology and imagery enter the play largely through Brutus's attempt "to dignify assassination . . . by lifting it to a level of rite and ceremony."[1] I argue, however, that human sacrifice is on everyone's lips in this play. Discussion and representation of ritual destruction of humans to appease the gods, and its ominous "preparation" in "holiday" gatherings, pervade the drama to such an extent, as chapter 8 will demonstrate, as to create a problem in interpretation of the play.[2] As G. Wilson Knight has shown about the use of the images of "blood" or "love" in this work,[3] would-be ritual sacrifice, that "savage spectacle," creates a leitmotif that goes well beyond Brutus's supposed political smokescreen, from the earliest moments in the drama. In this chapter, I hope to demonstrate Shakespeare's unfolding of this theme and argue that the playwright, in this play, took occasion to schematize the dangers of man's reversion to the savage in a crisis of rule in Rome. *Julius Caesar*, thus, is tragic, but it is also about tragedy. Shakespeare's picture of leveling, in some ways darker than that of *King Lear*, if initially ambiguous, is ultimately Dionysian, quintessentially tragic. It pictures struggle as an annihilator of distinctions. In this drama, Shakespeare's initial ambivalence yields to mirroring rivalry and random group violence that triumph over all conciliation and communion.

The play opens with a puzzle that has two "readings," like an optical illusion. Shakespeare's stage presents either the last moment of tragic disintegration or the first of ritual healing: crowd-forming, the grouping of people who then can focus "universal" energy on gods, heroes, and victims. Shakespeare introduces the ambivalence of ritual gathering, sanctioned or unsanctioned, unanimous or variously biased, in his first words. Two tribunes, Marullus and Flavius, confront citizens lacking the "sign" of their "profession" (1.1.4), a group of people who enjoy the anonymity of "holy-day" gear. The tribunes simply do not know from their "best apparel . . . best attire" (1.1.8, 48) who these commoners are, and, as a result of this confusion, the cobbler is free to try his impertinence on them with holiday license:

> *Flavius.* Thou art a cobbler, art thou?
> *Cobbler.* Truly, sir, all that I live by is with the awl. (1.1.20–21)

Indeed the cobbler lives with the shoe hammer or "awl" but also the "all," the crowd of individuals in the defilade of indistinguishable clothing.

Flavius recognizes a problem in rule, and he indirectly seeks an admission from the cobbler that he has usurped the tribunes' own authority to administer and represent the tribes: "Why dost thou lead these men about the streets" (1.1.28)? The cobbler accepts the imputation in his comic reply: "Truly, sir, to wear out their shoes, to get myself into more work." But the tribunes are not satisfied that he has such a mercenary goal.

When the cobbler finally relents and admits "we make holiday to see Caesar and rejoice in his triumph," Marullus's "golden" speech, the first of many in the play, voices tribunal objections to the citizens' behavior: unauthorized assembly and assumption of power, disloyalty in choosing to glorify Caesar's victory over Pompey's sons just as they rejoiced in Pompey's own victories. The workers stand accused of being unable to distinguish who they are celebrating, but also of being indistinguishable one from the other. Thus, Marullus's speech returns to the problems of wearing indecipherable clothing that disguises social and political identity. He says,

> You blocks, you stones, you worse than senseless things!
> O you hard hearts, you cruel men of Rome.
> Knew you not Pompey? Many a time and oft
> Have you climbed up to walls and battlements,
> To tow'rs and windows, yea, to chimney tops,
> Your infants in your arms, and there have sat
> The livelong day, with patient expectation,
> To see great Pompey pass the streets of Rome.
> And when you saw his chariot but appear,
> Have you not made an universal shout,

> That Tiber trembled underneath her banks
> To hear the replication of your sounds
> Made in her concave shores?
> And do you now put on your best attire?
> And do you now cull out a holiday?
>
> (1.1.35–49)

Marullus's badgering the crowd with an anaphoric sequence of rhetorical questions, like a schoolmaster, expresses the threat that a "popular" Caesar might pose to his tribunal power, but the image of the Tiber trembling "beneath her banks" also suggests "flooding" of an urban crowd, as "you blocks, you stones" suggest its weaponry.

The audience, with Flavius's help, may well assume that these artisans have joined up to break laws "upon a laboring day" (1.1.4), and thus it is surprised, I think, when Marullus responds to his own seemingly unanswerable question about "culling out a holiday" privately to Flavius: "You know it is the feast of Lupercal" (1.1.67). Holiday garb is the proper dressing up of the "all" on the day of the wolf sacred to Mars, Rome's most ancient fertility rite. The tribunes are denying ritual remembrance of Rome's primeval sacrificial rite[4] in dispersing the commoners and denuding the statues, for which they are later "put to silence" (1.2.283), apparently by Caesar. Thus this crowd-forming can imply both social disintegration and ritual healing, but the former becomes more prominent. Shakespeare goes on to mirror the difficulty the tribunes experience in distinguishing individual plebeians later when Lucius, as I have shown, fails to identify elements of the patrician conspiracy.

In the opening of the second act, when Brutus asks Lucius if he knows by sight the men with Cassius at the door, the boy responds emphatically,

> No, Sir. Their hats are plucked about their ears
> And half their faces buried in their cloaks,
> That by no means I may discover them
> By any mark of favor.
>
> (2.1.73–75)

The attractive and understating Lucius in his second longest speech in the play calls attention to the problem of undiscoverable identity, the phrase "mark of favor" echoing Flavius's reference to the absence of the "sign / Of your profession" in the opening words of the play. Brutus rues the necessity of such disguise, required protection even in the dark.

> O conspiracy,
> Sham'st thou to show thy dang'rous brow by night,
> When evils are most free? O, then by day
> Where wilt thou find a cavern dark enough
> To mask thy monstrous visage?
>
> (2.1.77–81)

What is the problem? Is Brutus solely concerned with detection? For Brutus, shame seems to reside in resigning self-control in favor of group will in ritual or conspiracy.

For Brutus and stoical Portia at least, self-control is the highest human achievement in its pristine individuality. In crowds it is lost. Mass will then rules. In this very scene Cato's daughter warns her husband not "to dare the vile contagion of the night" (2.1.265). She tells Brutus that he suffers from a mental disorder, and she suspects it concerns the fellow conspirators, "Some six or seven, who did hide their faces / Even from darkness" (2.1.277–78). As in other plays, contagion, plague, all catching sicknesses, become metaphors both for dissolving identity in a crowd and for a crowd's regaining health by destroying a human victim—that is, losing deathly sickness by passing it on. Thus at the end of this long scene, Caius Ligarius can "discard" his illness only if someone picks up his discard. Sick men become whole by means of "some whole that we must make sick" (2.1.328). This aristocratic crowd seems to be on its way to perform human sacrifice, but it could well be a lynch-mob.

As the plebeians were setting out to an abortive ritual on the Lupercal, a month later, on the Ides of March, the conspirators set off to a ritual sacrifice of Caesar that fails. Brutus urges the conspirators to remain unmoved in ceremonial "dismemberment" of Caesar:

> Let's be sacrificers, but not butchers, Caius.
> We all stand up against the spirit of Caesar,
> And in the spirit of men there is no blood.
> O that we then could come by Caesar's spirit
> And not dismember Caesar! But, alas,
> Caesar must bleed for it. And, gentle friends,
> Let's kill him boldly, but not wrathfully;
> Let's carve him as a dish fit for the gods,
> Not hew him as a carcass fit for hounds.
>
> (2.1.166–74)

Brutus here specifically calls for what he later fears Antony will see as the "savage spectacle" (3.1.223) of ritual human sacrifice. And although in his exhortation he seems to wish that Caesar had no blood, he will need blood for his ceremony. When Caesar has been murdered, he will call for a symbolic wash:

> Stoop, Romans, stoop,
> And let us bathe our hands in Caesar's blood
> Up to the elbows and besmear our swords.
>
> (3.1.105–7)

Certainly Brutus does not intend to terrify the citizens, as Cassius may take it, but to show them that the murder was unanimously approved and properly performed and therefore, in a sense, a guiltless ritual, all in the name of "Peace, freedom, and liberty!" (3.1.110). Peace will always be restored when such a ceremonial sacrifice—human, animal, or vegetable—includes all. As Brutus puts it, "we shall be called purgers, not murderers" (2.1.180).

This proposed human sacrifice fails and magically becomes just another in a long line of collective murders because it lacks "general" sanction, notably among Caesar's faction, that includes generals, Mark Antony, Octavius, and Lepidus, but also among the citizens themselves—the general mass of people. At the end of this act, Shakespeare presents a gruesome parody of the assassination of Caesar in the destruction of Cinna the poet by a pro-Caesar crowd of citizens. And so one is returned to a picture of a massive force of plebeians—the "blocks," the "stones" of Rome—in action.

In general, critics have pictured the sacrificial imagery of Brutus as well as that of Mark Antony as conscious—even rational—political gesturing,[5] but I think the inclusion of the parallel assassination of Cinna in the play inevitably calls attention to the unconscious and irrational in such activity. For example, the plebeians find absurd reasons for destroying the wrong Cinna. The ostensible object of the questioning, Cinna the Poet's dwelling, his marital status, and profession, are all immaterial. The group has made note of his name, and he must die. Says the first plebeian after his true, and politically benign, identity is revealed, "It is no matter; his name's Cinna! Pluck but his name out of his heart" (3.3.33). Innocent hearts carry guilt well.

In using arbitrary excuses for destroying Cinna, the plebeians echo Brutus's consciously irrational prosecution of Caesar in soliloquy (2.1.10). Brutus knew he was mentally trying his friend and general for crimes that he had not committed:

> And to speak truth of Caesar,
> I have not known when his affections swayed
> More than his reason.
>
> (2.1.19–21)

His peremptory procedure of condemnation finds utterance in his denunciation of the crime of "ambition" in his speech to the commoners, and the term is snapped up by Antony in his most effective sarcasm. No character lacks ambition, as Antony implies, nor can it be measured. Hugh Richmond once said about Brutus's mental prosecution of Caesar that "No system of justice has ever yet succeeded in effectively evaluating criminal intent,"[6] but here there are no systems of justice, merely a mechanism that exists prior to law and survives only in the absence of superior law of courts and police and international restraint. It works by "savage" necessity, squelching all sympathy for a "notable" victim. As Brutus puts it, "As fire drives out fire, so pity pity" (3.1.171). Group violence focuses on the person who is most visible for any sort of reason, for his race, his disability, or, here, the name of the poet (ironically a friend to Caesar) and its accidental identity with the name of a conspirator. In neither collective murder are "reasons" and reason sufficient.

As he does so often, Shakespeare draws a laugh in an otherwise grisly scene of destruction, here, as seen before, when Fourth Plebeian repeats "Tear him for his bad verses!" (3.3.30). The poet, especially the dramatic poet subjects himself to being "torn" by his audience, that crowd, often unanimous in its negative or positive response, perhaps in the Globe Theatre at the moment of reception of a newly staged version of *The Tragedy of Julius Caesar*. One is reminded of the poet's sometime fate late in the play in another comic moment when the intrusive peacemaker, the "cynic" poet, is rudely dismissed by Brutus with "what should the wars do with these jigging fools? / Companion, hence!" (4.3.137–38). The wars have a great deal to do with jigging fools, like our dramatist-poet, Shakespeare, after they happen. Behold the circumstance of the play in a modern language, a circumstance suggested by Cassius's oddly sanguine rhetorical question,

> How many ages hence
> Shall this our lofty scene be acted over
> In states unborn and accents yet unknown!
>
> (3.1.111–13)

Therefore the cynic poet's exclusion seems unfair as well. Suffering the fate of the self-appointed policeman, he too is being ganged up on and torn for his bad verse.

As a poet like Cinna can become the arbitrary focus of a crowd often for the worse, so can an aging ruler, suffering perhaps from infertility, deaf in one ear, experiencing a sequence of attacks of "falling sickness," a "divine" ailment he metaphorically passes on to his murderers. While Caesar may or may not plan to destroy senatorial power, as ruling consul he inevitably exposes himself to destruction for the good of all in times of strife. Like the North Star to which he pompously likens himself, he enjoys ultimate visibility, as Brutus does in the opening scene of act 5, when he suggests he would commit suicide to avoid being led in triumph. Performance of the ritual "play" of victory of the triumph and its unanimous applause was my point of departure in the play, warning that a rhythm of destroying leaders and vendetta and emulation precedes the very action of this drama.

From the first moment of this play, on the occasion of the celebration of Caesar's victory over Pompey's sons, the audience is treated to the cycles of Roman internecine destruction of political leaders, the group murder of its titular hero constituting a mere moment in the play's pattern of strife. Shakespeare's audience knows that Brutus is wrong before the battle of Philippi when he states "this same day / Must end that work the ides of March begun" (5.1.112–13). Brutus wants his own human self-sacrifice to contain all the awful violence, but the Elizabethan audience knows that Caesar's murder did not begin a new process. If one argued that the murder of Caesar set in motion the violence that follows for nearly three full acts, one could answer that the assassination of Pompey in Egypt immediately set in motion that violence. The memory of murdered Pompey never goes unmentioned in *Julius Caesar* for long, and his violent drama is the point of departure of the play's action.

Pompey's career is specifically identified with that of Caesar in the bleeding statue—which suggests the folklore of unsatisfied revenge or bad blood—and with that of Cassius, the hatcher of the plot to kill Caesar, in his being "(As Pompey was) . . . compelled to set / Upon one battle all our liberties" (5.1.74–75). To maintain the connection between the assassination of Caesar and that of Pompey, Pompey's porch or theater is mentioned as the location of the conspirators' first meeting place no less than three times in twenty-seven lines (1.3.126–52). Shakespeare's audience, however, also knows that the sequence of political murders in Rome, which began nearly a century before Pompey's death with the senatorial group murder of the tribune Tiberius Gracchus, continues up until the suicide of Cleopatra and Antony. Eventually the *pax Romana* of Caesar Augustus and Tiberius provides a platform for the life and death of Jesus. Shakespeare himself has provided an odd trilogy spanning the period in *Julius Caesar, Antony and Cleopatra,* and *Cymbeline*,[7] where the audience gradually, and with much pagan mythographic and other foreshadowing, enters the Christian era.

As in the case of Pompey's death, violence never contains itself in the ritual death of Julius Caesar. "Bad blood" augments vendetta arithmetically until, in the play, one seems to be concerned only with numbers. When Messala reports that "Octavius, Antony, and Lepidus / Have put to death an hundred senators" (4.3.174–75), an impassive Brutus replies, "Therein our letters do not well agree. / Mine speak of seventy senators that died / By their proscriptions, Cicero being one." Brutus seems abstracted here, as he does when he twice allows himself to receive the report of Portia's suicide by swallowing fire. One guesses that he is not himself, not well in health. As Portia herself puts it to Lucius, he went "sickly forth" (2.4.14) to the capitol on the Ides of March. Who did he become but a Caesar among Caesars, as the cobbler became a tribune among tribunes? Brutus becomes part of the conspiracy by a process of emulation on which Cassius consciously capitalizes.

From the first, "poor Brutus, with himself at war" (1.2.46), is aware of a violent internal disruption, later describing his soul, as I have noted, as "A little kingdom" suffering the "nature of an insurrection" (2.1.68). But he does not understand his internal political disorder, nor that his soul is mirroring the uprising and leveling about to occur in Rome. He employs a mirror image with Cassius, who gradually attempts to "inspire" him with desire to imitate Caesar. To Cassius's "can you see your face?" (1.2.51), Brutus says, "No, Cassius; for the eye sees not itself / But by reflection, by some other things." If one leaves out his ultimate qualification in this observation, one has a clear metaphor for one way of gaining self-knowledge. One sees one's own character in the reactions (mirror) to it. But "by some other things" is a puzzling addendum, as it suggests the possibility that one could imitate others. Cassius capitalizes on Brutus's "reflection" metaphor, proposing a sequence of possible mirror images for Brutus, from the Roman in general, to Cassius himself, climaxing with Caesar.

First he points out that "many of the best respect in Rome / ... Have wished that noble Brutus had his eyes" (1.2.59–62). Cassius suggests that these people have hoped he were not blind, but also that they have desired that Brutus identify with them: they have hoped that Brutus would only see through their eyes and understand problems that existed in Rome the way they did. When Brutus complains "That you would have me seek into myself / For that which is not in me" (1.2.64–65), Cassius is now ready to refer to the "other thing," to Caesar. Caesar the *imperator* still may be "outside" Brutus, but not for long. Cassius now suggests that Brutus consider himself (Cassius) as Brutus's mirror. Only half in jest, he replies:

> Therefore, good Brutus, be prepared to hear;
> And since you know you cannot see yourself
> So well as by reflection, I, your glass,
> Will modestly discover to yourself
> That of yourself which you yet know not of.
> (1.2.66–70)

Cassius's apparent admission that he is manipulating Brutus and his use of "therefore" to begin his "answer" have perplexed editors and directors alike, who tend to transform Brutus's complaint into an aside. But Cassius and Brutus are not uniformly attentive to others' words. "Therefore" seems merely a "logical" term licensing Cassius to continue his emotional appeal for emulation of Caesar.

Directors can cast Cassius as a villain here, with leering asides, mesmerizing noble Brutus, and when he is alone delivering with false self-deprecation his plan to forge letters to get more than a little fire from Brutus, but such procedure would belie the sympathetic lieutenant to Brutus of act 5. The final act reveals a man of high intellect who refuses to resist morally what he has decided is the sole, immutable law of human nature, the law of inexorable rivalry, factional strife, and conspiracy, that is, mutability. And Shakespeare lends him a tragic death that ironically reflects his obsession. Overlooking the battle of Philippi, he is presented as witnessing his friend Titinius surrounded by friends and given the wreath of victory.

With Pindarus's help, however, he mistakes a happy reunion for the slaughter of his comrade at the hands of a group of hostile cavalry. With truly "thick" (5.3.21) vision, Cassius can only "picture" worlds of conscious rivalry and collective murder. In his early attempt to enlist Brutus in the first act, Cassius is seen as a believer seeking, somewhat underhandedly, a convert. But how else does one cause human conversion? Profoundly cynical, Cassius lacks Brutus's idealism, yet it is Brutus's idealism that keeps him from narrowly analyzing internal and external disorder.

Cassius moves with Brutus on to a narration of a double-dare with Caesar, where, in part, because of Caesar's falling sickness, Cassius is victor.

> For once, upon a raw and gusty day,
> The troubled Tiber chafing with her shoes,
> Caesar said to me, 'Dar'st thou, Cassius, now
> Leap in with me into this angry flood
> And swim to yonder point?' Upon the word,
> Accoutred as I was, I plungèd in
> And bade him follow. So indeed he did.
> The torrent roared, and we did buffet it
> With lusty sinews, throwing it aside
> And stemming it with hearts of controversy.
> (1.2.100–109)

Cassius, in his "will-less" and instantaneous response to Caesar's dare, as well as his head start, has plunged into a symbolic flood of envy and emulation of which he is fully aware.

Thus, with consummate oratorical skill, Cassius leads Brutus into contemplation of like emulation of Caesar. If he succeeds, Brutus will gradually lose himself, his difference from his friend and rival, Caesar. His "mettle may be wrought / From that it is disposed" (1.2.306–307), and he will be at one with the conspiracy, as well as a mirror of Caesar. His metal will have melted[8] into a common pool. Cassius takes pains to tell Brutus that he is a "modest" rhetorical mirror here and as they part when he says "I am glad / That my weak words have struck but thus much show / Of fire from Brutus" (1.2.175–77), but Shakespeare lends his monosyllabic words an emphatic Senecan amble:[9]

> 'Brutus,' and 'Caesar.' What should be in that 'Caesar'?
> Why should that name be sounded more than yours?
> Write them together: yours is as fair a name.
> Sound them: it doth become the mouth as well.
> Weigh them: it is as heavy. Conjure with 'em:
> 'Brutus' will start a spirit as soon as 'Caesar.'
> (1.2.142–47)

Clearly, Cassius is not asking Brutus to be a co-conspirator but dictator of the conspiracy, a role he adopts, Caesar of the senatorial party.

Brutus seems unconscious[10] of his mirroring Julius Caesar even at the moment that he performs the same grandstand rhetorical act. At the end of his great speech to the commoners from the pulpit, he says, with Sophoclean irony, "I have the same dagger for myself when it shall please my country to need my death" (3.2.44–46). Such will soon be the case at Philippi. These words forcibly recall Caesar's speech and action after his fainting spell at the Lupercal. In Casca's rough words, Caesar "plucked me ope his doublet and offered them his throat to cut" (1.2.262).

The identity of the two actions is not lost on the plebeians. Their response is:

ALL. Live, Brutus! live! live!
1. *Plebeian.* Bring him with triumph home unto his house.
2. *Plebeian.* Give him a statue with his ancestors.
3. *Plebeian.* Let him be Caesar.
4. *Plebeian.*   Caesar's better parts
   Shall be crowned in Brutus. (3.2.47–51)

Mention of crowning, the occasion of Caesar's offer of self-sacrifice, underlines the ironic simplicity of the proposed identification. Response among the crowd of citizens to both republican gestures—Caesar's refusal of the crown and Brutus's panegyric of political freedom—is uniformly "monarchic," but such a quality is not unknown to the senators.

Brutus has become the new Caesar for the moment, dictating like Caesar what is often unfortunate policy to Cassius and the other conspirators, who "grace his heels" (3.1.120), like the "throng" that followed "Caesar at the heels" (2.4.34). Ordering that Mark Antony be spared and that troops be committed at Philippi over Cassius's sound objections that these actions are unsafe resembles Caesar's intransigent manner in dealing with the requests concerning security of his wife, or the soothsayer, or Artemidorus. Brutus comes, furthermore, to sound very much like Caesar in self-praise. Responding to what he calls Cassius's "threats," he says

> I am armed so strong in honesty
> That they pass by me as the idle wind,
> Which I respect not.
>   (4.3.67–69)

Like Caesar, he refers to himself in the third person in demanding ill-earned money from Cassius to pay his troops:

> When Marcus Brutus grows so covetous
> To lock such rascal counters from his friends,
> Be ready, gods, with all your thunderbolts,
> Dash him to pieces!
>
> (4.3.79–82)

Like Caesar, he pictures himself as a direct object of the gods' interests, a center of attention of the "heavens." Yet Brutus fails to recognize the similarity. Before the battle of Philippi, Caesar's rather accommodating ghost introduces himself as "Thy evil spirit, Brutus" (4.3.282). Without reference to the content of this statement, Brutus simply asks, "Why com'st thou?" The suggestion that Caesar's ghost might be his own evil spirit—that his identity is one with Caesar's—does not puzzle him perhaps because he is not fully aware of what has been said.

In Elizabethan revenge tragedy, the ghost of the prior victim may appear not in front of his murderer, like Macbeth, but strictly in front of his avenger, like Hamlet. Caesar's ghost appears to both in the same person. Brutus will simultaneously become Caesar's avenger and his punished murderer in his own suicide—and by the same sword. His identity here with Caesar will be final and complete. The man who sacrificed Caesar will be sacrificed as the man who sacrificed Pompey was sacrificed. After his death, Antony's priestly glorification of the victim as the "noblest Roman of them all . . . 'This was a man!'" (5.5.68, 75) will closely follow his remarks on Caesar's death: "The most noble blood of all this world" (3.1.156), "Noble Caesar . . . Here was a Caesar! When comes such another?" (3.2.184, 252). In neither case, however, does Antony's oration lead to the peace that should come with ritual funerals. Vendetta lives on, as the eventual rise of Sextus Pompeius in *Antony and Cleopatra* witnesses. "Bad blood" again has been spilt, even by self-slaughter, and Antony's Orphic delivery can only "move / The stones of Rome" (3.2.229–30)—unbeknownst to him in this case—to more violence. In his elegy to Brutus, Antony absolves him of "envy" (5.5.70), and I believe that he is correct. Artemidorus knows that Caesar died in the "teeth of emulation" (2.3.14), emulation that in Brutus's case was unconscious. Brutus knew he was not well, but he did not know why. His illness remained undiagnosed. Caesar's image remains Brutus's spirit for good and for evil, yet Caesar had priority. He was the unwavering model for emulation in a sick society in turmoil, as well as the human victim of would-be sacrificial knives.

Typically, Shakespeare in *Julius Caesar* develops several sorts of schematic parallels, around the major speeches, around philosophical divergence of Epicurian and Stoic, around similar scenes such as Brutus's debate with Portia and Caesar's with Calphurnia, or the two group murders. One theme he illuminates is human sacrifice. He paints a picture of rivalry, not of the comic or healing, but of the diseased sort that culminates in an absence of rule in the Roman streets and in the theaters and porches and steps frequented by the aristocracy. He also paints a picture of group-forming that is not cooperative or "pastoral" or even ritualistic, but irrational and violent, the central event being the destruction of Caesar, whose great powers in the state, as well as his physical disabilities, set him off and made him a center of attention. Caesar's own words confirm his place or "ordinance" in this volatile political situation. Only Caesar knows, in his intransigent way, that he is

> the Northern Star,
> Of whose true-fixed and resting quality
> There is no fellow in the firmament,
>
> (3.1.60–62)

while the conspirators, as Thomas Rymer once sardonically pointed out, "have no more in their heads than to wrangle about which is the East and West"[11] when they come in conference:

Decius. Here lies the east. Doth not the day break here?
Casca. No.
Cinna. O, pardon, sir, it doth; and yon grey lines
  That fret the clouds are messengers of day.
Casca. You shall confess that you are both deceived.
  Here, as I point my sword, the sun arises. . . .

(2.1.101–6)

Yet Caesar's flattery and self-flattery and his ensuing disregard for his special place and his own safety mark a disability of rule that mock even some of his last words: "These couchings and these lowly courtesies . . . turn preordinance and first decree / Into the lane of children" (3.1.36, 38–3). Deriding the kneeling senators' arranged appeal for the freedom of Publius Cimber—"Doth not Brutus bootless kneel?" (3.1.75)—Caesar is stabbed by Casca who calls for the end of all words, as I have shown: "Speak hands for me." As when the plebeians tear Cinna for his bad verses, Casca calls for the end of signifiers. Indeed he might, words making distinctions that no longer exist in the final stage of tragic disintegration.

PART 3
The Politics of Literary Borrowing and Exclusion

6

Publishing the Politics of Literary Expropriation: Lyly and Marlowe in *1 Henry IV*

If Shakespeare represents leveling as, in part, accompanying a breakdown in the distinctions that words make, the reestablishment of language, as I have shown, offers a solution. Publication of a problem in rule may restore peace and order in the universe, including the stage. The single line "Tear him for his bad verses," for example, publicizes the vulnerability of the poet and seeks to cure a problem by exposing it, as do Shakespeare's many open references to competition among playwrights and play companies, practically unheard of on the twentieth-century stage. Rivalry among poets and expropriation of words were admitted realities of Shakespeare's life. Eight of his 154 sonnets in Thorpe's sequence deal directly with poetic rivalry with one or more of his contemporaries. But the bitterness and "misprision" of poetic competition were "cauterized" by the very inflammatory self-advertisement of Shakespeare's literary quarrels. In fact, only when controversy over a text, such as *Julius Caesar*, survived its maker did the process of rivalry and leveling of the poet's words play itself out in all its violence, as shown in chapter 8. In his own time, for various purposes, Shakespeare openly borrowed many words including those of his brilliant contemporary poets and prosers, perhaps most notably in *1 Henry IV*, because borrowing, in this play, helps "schematize," or structure, the drama itself.

Following E. M. W. Tillyard's seminal remarks on Shakespeare's use of a congeries of idioms in the *Henriad*, critics have noted that, in keeping with the national and "epical"[1] quality of the second tetralogy, Shakespeare presents a compendium of speakers of English.[2] Bolingbroke and son normally deliver a heavily metaphoric, regal, English blank verse akin to some of the "voices" of the sonnets. Francis the Waiter—when he gets a chance—speaks an early version of Cockney prose. Glendower speaks perfect Welsh sometimes in a musical hyperbolic English. Douglas speaks a clipped and sturdy Scots-English. Fluellen, Macmorris, and Jamy speak an odd assortment of dialects; Katherine speaks French and learner's—future immigrant's—English. Thus the nascent British Empire with its assorted accents and versions of imperial English may be contained, in some sense, by Shakespeare's stage.

Tillyard, however, also points out that Shakespeare borrowed the idiom of rival poets in his great epic tetralogy, notably Samuel Daniel. In this chapter, I argue that Shakespeare helps structure one of the four plays, 1 Henry IV, out of two radically different "speaking" versions of miles gloriosus, Harry Percy and Sir John Falstaff, who separately speak Marlovian blank verse and the prose style that came to be known as "euphuism."[3] In this way, Shakespeare publicizes his debt and exposes the process of literary expropriation in which he is involved. In having his Hotspur and Jack speak in the brilliant, justaposed idioms of his two major contemporary influences in poetry and prose, Christopher Marlowe and John Lyly, Shakespeare improbably links the two figures—given their difference in age, habits, and attitudes—as soldiers who fabricate their tales according to heroic imaginings on demand, but also as polar "literary" voices. Therefore, in 1 Henry IV, one hears not only a compendium of ethnic language, but also a "dialogue" that opposes the leading stars on Shakespeare's own literary horizon in London intellectual circles and on the English stage. Juxtaposing this odd couple of characters and influences helps structure a play that—thanks to its chronicle origins—is likely to seem "loose" or episodic.

Like all professional writers, Shakespeare gradually absorbed his influences by a "political" process that begins with imitation—even quoting—and ends—or begins to end—with a tendency to parody or burlesque. In his well-known attack on Shakespeare in the first published reference to the young actor, playwright, and poet, in *Groats-VVorth of Witte*, Robert Greene went out of his way to note that Shakespeare imitated his contemporaries—one presumes Greene himself, Lyly, and other so-called University Wits, but also the high tragedians, Kyd and Marlowe. What he says, however, merely reminds one of the universal process of literary expropriation that Shakespeare so often represents and, indeed, plays out:

> there is an vpstart Crow, beautified with our feathers, that with his *Tygers hart wrapt in a Players hyde*, supposes he is as well able to

bombast out a blanke verse as the best of you: and beeing an absolute *Iohannes fac totum*, is in his owne conceit the onely Shake-scene in a countrey.[4]

If "shaking scenes" implies random play construction, and beautifying with others' feathers, plagiarism, tigerish bombasting out a blank verse suggests the elementary mode that Shakespeare arrived at in his high tragedy, partly with the help of Marlowe's innovation, a debt Shakespeare publicly admits. In his plays, to my knowledge, he directly quotes only one line of a contemporary poet's verse. In *As You Like It*, act 3, scene 5, line 81, Shakespeare's Phebe recalls that "dead shepherd's" "saw of might": "Who ever lov'd that lov'd not at first sight?" from Marlowe's moralization of a recognition scene in *Hero and Leander* (2.436).[5] This passage graciously reminds the audience of Shakespeare's admiration for Marlowe, though the latter is not named, and it demonstrates the elementary form of literary expropriation, direct quoting. At the far end of a history of influence, however, in perhaps the most complex version of authorial borrowing conceivable, the author treats his original admired text, as I have said, with irony.

Shakespeare's editors, notably Steevens and Strachey,[6] early noted that Shakespeare parodies Marlowe in the lines from the old play Hamlet requires the First Player to deliver in act 2, scene 2, "Aeneas' tale to Dido," a version, I believe, of several passages in Marlowe's *The Tragedy of Dido, Queen of Carthage*.[7] For example, at one moment, Marlowe had tried out onomatopoeic alliteration in describing the hyperbolical, perilously close to burlesque, flooring the Trojan King merely by means of the wind created by Pyrrhus's sword rushing through the air, so far removed from the abrupt Virgilian stabbing in the *Aeneid*, book 2. Marlowe writes that Pyrrhus

> Whiskt his sword about
> And with the wind thereof the King fell down.
> (11.23–24)

The reiterate "w" provides an imitation of the sound of the sword's rapid movement.

Hamlet's First Player, however, says,

> with the whiff and wind of his fell sword
> Th' unnervèd father falls.
> (2.2.461–63)

Marlowe's honest attempt at sound effects is made ludicrous, I believe, in the alliterative formula "with the whiff and wind," and the subsequent "fell" and "father falls" is parodic. Seeming stiff and antique for the times, these lines produce what Sir Philip Sidney called, in *The Defence of Poetry,* English versifiers' "coursing of a letter, as if they were bound to follow the method of a dictionary" (117.17).[8] The lines burlesque Marlowe for effect. The ineffable humor, I feel, might well not be lost on Shakespeare's theater audience, much less on his poetic competitors, not merely for the Marlovian, hyperbolic image of King Priam bowled over by a puff of air, but for the "straining" poetry of its description. At least for aficionados of contemporary literary rivalry, Shakespeare's reference to Marlowe seems unmistakable.

Lying in between the process of direct quoting or close imitation and such burlesque, happily, lies the healthier realm of influence when Shakespeare's idiom sometimes seems to become an extension of the "dead shepherd's" content and style. As Sidney had warned about the nature of one's relationship to another author like Cicero, when submitting to influence, writers should take the initiative and "(as it were) devour them whole, and make them wholly theirs" (117.27–28). Shakespeare used Marlowe for the best in much of his blank verse, most notably to this ear in the speeches of Hotspur in his quest for unassailable honor.

Not only in its witty expression of his own overreaching, for example, but also in its hyperbolic blank verse that sometimes borders on burlesque of its own, Hotspur's first speeches in the play are Marlovian. First, he lies about refusing the crown hostages, "My liege, I did deny no prisoners" (1.3.29), then goes on to admit he "answered neglectingly, I know not what" (1.3.51) to a courtier on the battlefield. In his soldierly way, he describes this "dandified" and effeminate man—in his opinion—in hyperbolic terms. The very cut of his beard reminds Hotspur of acres of mown grain:

> and his chin new reaped
> Showed like a stubble land at harvest home.
> (1.3.34–35)

At this moment how far is the audience from the idiom of Marlowe's description of Hero's dress, as follows?

> Whereon was many a staine,
> Made with the blood of wretched Lovers slaine?
> (2.431)

The gap between a homely reality and an ideal vision teeters on the edge of bathos and creates rare poetic energy.

Alone with the conspirators later in this scene, Hotspur warms to his theme of maintaining pristine glory in a world of men without equal:

> By heaven, methinks it were an easy leap
> To pluck bright honor from the pale-faced moon,
> Or dive into the bottom of the deep,
> Where fathom line could never touch the ground,
> And pluck up drownèd honor by the locks,
> So he that doth redeem her thence might wear
> Without corrival all her dignities.
> (1.3.201–7)

This passage seems to amplify the ill-fated imaginative flights of another superman, Faustus, who cries out near the end,

> O, I'le leape up to my God, who puls me downe?
> (2.225)

Not only Hotspur's actions but his very mode of expressing his thoughts convey such excitation and "poetic exaggeration that Worcester dryly counters with,

> He apprehends a world of figures here.
> (1.3.209)

In Marlovian fashion, "figures," "figments of imagination," are meshed with rhetorical tropes, such as hyperbole and catachresis, "figures" that encode those dreams with such poetic excitement and exert such influence on Shakespeare, and openly so.

When Hotspur finally meets his corrival, Prince Hal, and his Maker, so to speak, simultaneously, Shakespeare's tragic hero in this history play delivers his plight in Marlovian blank verse—what Jonson called "Marlowes mighty line"[9]—augmented with an echo of the alliterative verse of antique English heroic poetry:

> O Harry, thou hast robbed me of my youth!
> I better brook the loss of brittle life
> Than those proud titles thou hast won of me.
> They wound my thoughts worse than thy sword my flesh.
> But thoughts the slaves of life, and life time's fool,
> And time, that takes survey of all the world,
> Must have a stop. O, I could prophesy,
> But that the earthy and cold hand of death
> Lies on my tongue. No, Percy, thou art dust,
> and food for—*(Dies.)*
>
> (5.4.76–85)

Hal sardonically completes his thought, "for worms," but adds "brave Percy," as Shakespeare could have said "brave Marlovian Hotspur." The image of death laying an "earthy and cold" hand on his tongue is evocation of the sensation of death that Marlowe so often strove to represent. In fact, Marlowe may remain the great English poet of the sensations of love and death, and if one were, hypothetically, to remove his influence, it would be difficult to imagine the shape Shakespeare's work would have taken. But the relationship of innovator and influenced poet is here not obscured, as so often, but clarified and published in Shakespeare's efforts to reproduce the dead shepherd's "might" in Hotspur's voice.

In prose, John Lyly's critical, antithetical style, I argue, provided Shakespeare with his leading model, and, in his references to this master, Shakespeare discloses a similar process of literary expropriation. Shakespeare never directly quotes Lyly in his plays, but he often employs Lyly's prose style so closely that it is hard to imagine the lines as anything but echoes of his senior contemporary. In *The Merchant of Venice*, for example, listen to Portia speak to her lady-servant Nerissa, albeit in blank verse, in balanced antithesis about morality to be drawn from observation of the animal kingdom:

> The crow doth sing as sweetly as the lark
> When neither is attended; and I think
> The nightingale, if she should sing by day
> When every goose is cackling, would be thought
> No better a musician than the wren.
> How many things by season seasoned are
> To their right praise and true perfection!
>
> (5.1.102–8)

If Shakespeare is here not quoting Lyly, in his antithesis, emphatic rhythms, and word echo, he is not devouring him whole either. This is high imitation. He provides, I feel, a picture of courtly language and matter that may reflect the euphuism he no doubt heard in Elizabeth's court and read in the works of Lyly, but he has not, I feel, fully incorporated the style in his Portia.

Lyly's prose style remains, in general, underrated, condemned as sinewless ornamentation, with exceptions,[10] almost from the day of Sidney's remarks in *The Defence of Poetry* about overuse of simile:

> Now for similitudes, in certain printed discourses, I think all herbarists, all stories of beasts, fowls, and fishes, are rifled up, that they come in multitudes to wait upon any of our conceits. (118.13–16)

By means of his examples from the animal, vegetable, and mineral worlds, however, and his insistent antithesis and word echo, I feel Lyly creates a magical unscientific world where all elements of nature join to argue against profligate young men, who, however, argue back with the natural world's own text wittily displaced. This "anatomy" of discourse provided a fundamental influence on Shakespeare throughout his career.

At the far end of the process of literary expropriation, there is parody of Lyly in Falstaff's voice in the mock counsel scene that foreshadows Hal's actual scenes with his father in act 3, scene 2, and, of course, act 4, scene 5 of *2 Henry IV*. In this vestigial play within a play, Shakespeare delivers a stylistic parody as well as burlesque of the moral of Lyly's original. Falstaff, like all stock comic soldiers, exaggerates and lies, but unlike Hotspur, he always seems at least dimly—humorously in all meanings of the word—conscious of his falsehood. Often the audience is warned by the fine critical distinctions that Falstaff makes in his antithetical prose. But he is also capable of burlesque of his own and by extension, Lyly's method:

> Harry, I do not only marvel where thou spendest thy time, but also how thou art accompanied. For though the camomile, the more it is trodden on, the faster it grows, yet youth, the more it is wasted, the sooner it wears. (2.4.380–84)

Like the titanic fan of Pyrrhus's sword, the concept of a plant that pushes up rapidly the more it is stepped on, cues Shakespeare's burlesque, but conceptual and stylistic parody also make their appearance. Part of the delight of this spoof comes from Falstaff's comparison of unlike things, an herb to the concept of adolescence, when Lyly always maintained correspondence and hierarchy—the common aromatic herb, camomile, to the uncommon flower, the violet. Furthermore, heavy antithesis and loping rhythm create a burlesque of euphuistic style.

In the famous passage in Lyly, the narrator of *Euphues: The Anatomy of Wit* looks awry at the wastrel hero's contempt for hard work and schooling by summarizing his own elitist argument:

> Too much studie both intoxicate their braynes, for (saye they) althoughe yron the more it is vsed the brighter it is, yet siluer with much wearing doth wast to nothing, though the Cammocke the more it is bowed the better it serueth, yet the bow the more it is bent & occupied, the weaker it waxeth, though the Camomill, the more it is trodden and pressed downe, the more it spreadeth, yet the violet the oftner it is handled and touched, the sooner it withereth and decayeth.[11]

Shakespeare's versions of Lyly's "herbarist" imagery—his alliteration, word echo, and antithesis all proclaiming quasi-Puritanical ethical postures—do not, however, disappear from his style once he has so effectively parodied them. I argue that melancholy Falstaff throughout this play and elsewhere—to what I suspect was the queen's delight—speaks in Lyly's prose style.

When Falstaff comes to challenge concepts of honor that have led his odd counterpart, Hotspur, into suicidal rebellion, he balances his echoing phrases and answers himself in euphuistic self-styled "catechism."

> Well, 'tis no matter; honor pricks me on. Yea, but how if honor prick me off when I come on? How then? Can honor set to a leg? No. Or an arm? No. Or take away the grief of a wound? No. Honor hath no skill in surgery then? No. What is honor? A word. What is that word honor? Air—a trim reckoning! Who hath it? He that died a Wednesday. Doth he feel it? No. Doth he hear it? No. 'Tis insensible then? Yea, to the dead. But will it not live with the living? No. Why? Detraction will not suffer it. Therefore I'll none of it. Honor is a mere scutcheon—and so ends my catechism. (5.1.129–39)

All Lyly's stylistic devices, from the pun on "prick" ("spur" and "write down") at the opening to the word echo of "none of" and "honor" at the close, are used to emphasize Falstaff's criticism of the supposed glory of rivalry and war. And though Puritan postures condemning the savage principle of "honor" that engenders suicide, dueling, and larger armed conflict were not always successful in England, nor so wittily expressed, Falstaff's euphuistic sermon serves to remind the audience of their moral validity. Falstaff successfully reduces war to needless physical danger. Through the juxtaposition of two *milites gloriosi* entirely at odds over the value of maintaining honor, Shakespeare has created another antithetical structure for a chronicle play that might otherwise look like "shaken scenes."

Again in soliloquy on the battlefield, seeing the exaggerated grin produced by Sir Walter Blunt's *rigor mortis*, Falstaff declaims in Lyly's idiom,

> Well, if Percy be alive, I'll pierce him. If he do come in my way, so; if he do not, if I come in his willingly, let him make carbonado of me. I like not such grinning honor as Sir Walter hath. Give me life; which if I can save, so; if not, honor comes unlooked for, and there's an end. (5.3.55–60)

The wordplay on "Percy" and "pierce him," the balance of phrases, tell a tale that equates honor with death, the very antinomy of the immortality Hotspur sought out.

In his echoes of his rivals, Shakespeare has announced to the world of the London stage his primary contemporary influences, and he has exposed the process of literary expropriation. Shakespeare has publicly devoured his influences in order to create parallels and juxtapositions that help structure his greatest chronicle play. At this moment in his career, as critics have long noted, Shakespeare was coming into contact with a younger rival, Ben Jonson, with whom he was to spend many years in the arena of public competition. But that rivalry, sometimes dangerous to both parties, took on an ideological tinge that affected the structure of some of Shakespeare's greatest efforts, such as *Twelfth Night* and *Julius Caesar*.

7

Exorcizing the Moral Jonsonian Citizen Comedy in Shakespeare's *Twelfth Night, or, What You Will*

Ever since the publication of Paul Mueschke's and Jeanette Fleisher's evocative article, "Jonsonian Elements in the Comic Underplot of *Twelfth Night*,"[1] critics have noted a cloud of literary rivalry over Ben Jonson's *Every Man in His Humour* of 1598 and Shakespeare's *Twelfth Night, or, What You Will* of 1600. While Shakespeare championed Jonson's work for the Lord Chamberlain's men, even insisted, apparently, on the performance of *Every Man in His Humour*, and played a principle role[2] its opening night, competition between the two friends—even public quarrels—proved inevitable, in part, for ideological reasons laid out in the Prologue Jonson attached to the 1616 Folio edition of that work. Jonson, an unequaled classicist, opposed folkloric elements in the genre at which Shakespeare excelled. And he opposed, apparently on neo-Aristotelian grounds that he rarely, in fact, followed, contamination of plot. As a critic, he was a generic purist both in the sense of condemning unrealistic, or unbelievable, elements of plot and any combination of two plots—or kinds of plot—in one play. Thus in this attached prologue, Jonson scoffs at both unmimetic and loose or multiple plot structure. He singles out the first and second tetralogies, "Yorke, and Lancasters long iarres" (11),[3] as unbelievably representing armies by "three rustie swords" (9) and importing a speaking chorus—who improbably "wafts you ore the seas"—to tell time and space in a multiple plot. However, Jonson saves his venom for romances, such as *Pericles*, *The Winter's Tale*, and *The Tempest*, with their fabulous storms, when the "tempestuous drumme / Rumbles" (19), and fabulous creatures. He closes the prologue with a lefthanded exhortation to his audience, as much aimed, I would guess at his friendly rival—creator of Caliban and

Ariel—as at the crowds he had come to think of as victimizing him: "You, that have so grac'd monsters, may like men" (30).

While Jonson dwells on the absence of *vraisemblance* and the unities of place and time, he implies throughout Shakespeare's signal failure to respect unity of action. A playwright, like Shakespeare, distracted by stage effects could never, he argues, stick to a single plot. Of course, sixteen years earlier, Shakespeare had already drawn Jonson's blood by various jibes[4] in *Twelfth Night*. In this play, Shakespeare spoofs Jonson specifically, but also, I argue, "generically" by fusing a quintessential Jonsonian rogue comedy with an improbable high fiction of the kind his friend would object to most. Furthermore, Shakespeare, within the play, "criticizes" the moral in Jonson's creation of staged scapegoats. By means of his use of the image of the "baited bear," Shakespeare implies that Jonson's stage exults in cruel "sacrifice" akin to hazing, but more violent. Thus, Jonson could witness this unholy "marriage," and specific and general criticism, on the stage of the company for whom he wrote his finest popular drama. Such fiery publication of literary quarrel on both sides seems to have branded and seared the tissue of their rivalry and quelled their tendency to violence in the competition. Thus, during Shakespeare's lifetime at least, the mutual animadversion of the rivals, if relentless and ideological, never degenerated into mutual harm and textual "dismemberment." Nevertheless, Shakespeare's singling out and "exorcizing" a perfect Jonsonian plot in *Twelfth Night* is by no means restrictively comic or even impartially "critical." Because the quarrel was public, however, it demanded the extension of controversy. Thus the competition preserved distinctions among the playwrights even to generating new forms for debate, such as the prologue and epilogue, and new generic configurations of Renaissance drama by means of generic contamination.

Looked at through Jonson's putative neo-Aristotelian eyes, *Twelfth Night* fuses two kinds of comic plot:[5] the hated romance or romantic comedy "upstairs," so to speak, and "downstairs" comedy, the new form now usually called citizen comedy. This form is also known as city, rogue, gull-victimization, gulling, or cony-catching comedy; satiric interlude; or, indeed, Jonsonian comedy of humors. Like newly arrived genres,[6] the nomenclature of that citizen comedy "downstairs" remains uncertain, but the essential morality, the sense of a representational, contemporary Elizabethan world, and the conventional expectations and emotional bias elicited by such a form are unusually fixed, thus placing it in direct—even comic—contrast to the form of the drama upstairs. Perhaps the most efficient way to expose the contamination might be to ask, if Sir Toby Belch, "downstairs," is Olivia's uncle, is it possible that Olivia's family name is Belch?

Shakespeare, I argue, in another public manifestation of his rivalry with Jonson, has allowed that kind of plot Jonson later called "mouldy"[7] to infect a "pure" imitation of Jonson's dramatic innovation. The upstairs plot, representing a genre redefined by Giraldi and others in *cinquecento* Italy, gratifies its audience in ways that Jonson always scorned. It is patently antimimetic, and its presence transforms the play into a forbidden generic alloy. As soon as Duke Orsino expresses his hope for a nausea that will carry him out of a state of love—"that surfeiting, / The appetite may sicken, and so die" (1.1.2–3)—the audience, thanks to its "love interest," is prepared to hope for—nay, demand—inevitable marriage. In that happy state, the partners will dwell in a timeless state of "happily ever after" (one concluding formula of fairy tale). The obstacles to such hoped-for marriage will be conventional romance-plot motifs: half-explained riddles, transvestite disguise, mistaken identity, ring plot, and an elaborate "obstructional" tragicomical recognition scene. Storms at sea and accident, twins, and coincidence will focus the emotional demand for neat providential resolution. Jonson knew about emotional bias in the audience, and perhaps it helped develop his antipathy to high romance, because as Wayne Booth, a latter-day neo-Aristotelian, says about such a genre, everything is simply too easy: "We are made to desire certain good things for certain good characters, and then our desires are gratified."[8]

Furthermore, when the audience realizes that the second scene takes place on the shore of Illyria,[9] it knows that it is in "no place"—a symbolic eastern Mediterranean locus no more verifiable than that seacoast of a land-locked Bohemia Jonson objected to in his conversation with William Drummond of Hawthornden—and at "no time," just as that initial formula of fairy tale, "once upon a time," emphatically implies its opposite, "never." As my so-called "upstairs" plot unfolds, the audience anxiously watches two dominant female characters, with quasi-anagrammatical names, Olivia and Viola, the female female and the tomboy, move through conventional trial toward a ritual group marriage in a land of potential nightmare suddenly—jarringly—resolved into a happy dream, by providential ending.

The moral, for Jonson, remains unclear. This plot (and this kind of plot) is most venerable, and like all romance, it resists much formalist elucidation. Shakespeare has preserved on the stage a story of his Olivia and Viola that suffered minor change over the millennia—immediately traceable back to Barnabe Rich's Renaissance tale "Of Apolonius and Silla," and the anonymous play *Sir Clyomon and Clamydes,* but also back to Italian tragicomedy, medieval sources, Greek romance, Latin comedy, Greek new comedy, perhaps even back to a hazy prehistory of Canaanite folktale. For Jonson's purposes, it is thoroughly moldy. This upstairs plot provides a timeless initiation rite for marriage on the stage, shared by design with the audience, and yet it haunts a perfect Jonsonian artifact.

Jonson designed his peculiar late Elizabethan and early Jacobean dramatic form, which reached its height, at least according to principles of generic purity, in *The Alchemist,* to be the most clearly "moral" as well as up-to-date of theater. In his prologue to *Every Man in His Humour,* he argues that his brand of comedy "would show an Image of the times, / And sport with humane[10] follies, not with crimes."[11] The genre should force the audience into "laughing" at its "popular errors." By authorial intention, an overpowering sense of the present and of the presence of folly will remind the audience of its own foolishness and affectation, and its members will be pleasantly purged of vice, as Aristotle himself might have suggested in his "lost" book on comedy.[12] "Image of the times" requires that the plot unfold in the locale of its literary origin and first audience, the contemporary city, Venice or London, of the turn of the seventeenth century, place requiring elaborate topical reference. Although the sometime beast fable or satiric naming of characters may seem to belie this point, the play is essentially representational, mimetic of the "day."

That Jonson would have comedy "sport with humane follies, not with crimes," moreover, applies both to the creator of the plot and to the con man or men at its center. First of all, the playwright must not combine laughter with felony and thereby teach a demonic morality. But the writer's surrogate on the stage, the central trickster, who, in a sense, creates the plot, must enjoy the baiting and trapping of folly, not crime. In a typical citizen comedy like *Volpone,* the audience becomes emotionally biased in favor of the con artists, in this case, Volpone himself and Mosca, organizers of the entrapment for gain and amusement of a sequence of well-deserving "gulls."[13] Of course, those gulls must not be criminal, but foolish, acquisitive out of some sort of warm-blooded vanity, or our rogues themselves would be "sporting" with crime when more drastic measures are "morally" demanded. Furthermore, the gulls must deserve their fate through their own vanity and affectation, or then they would be relative innocents with whom it would be a crime to sport, and emotional bias would swerve. All punishment in the plot must be apt. Wayne Booth helps explain the jarring severity of the tricksters' comeuppance in *Volpone*, I think, when he points out that

> the grasping but witty Volpone can keep us on his side so long as his victims are more grasping and less witty than he, but as soon as the innocent victims, Celia and Bonario, come on stage, the quality of the humor changes; we no longer delight unambiguously in his triumphs.[14]

Whether or not Celia and Bonario are entirely innocent, there is a predictable swerve in the audience's appreciation of the con men who gull them. Jonsonian citizen comedy initially sets in motion a series of confidence games victimizing gulls whose follies and affectations require chastisement in a citified world intermittently lorded over by admirable parasites, indeed, super-tricksters. The audience's emotional bias, until it is too late, remains on the side of those who "sport with folly." Ultimately, the con artists end up conning themselves, overreaching in the Marlovian mode, and they lose some of the audience's sympathy.

Typical of Jonson, in *Volpone*, gullibility is allied to human greed. Corbaccio is an old man hoping to be made young by a younger man's (Volpone's) death and the unequal (and unjust) distribution of his great wealth. The merchant Corvino can be talked into bartering his young wife's affections for an inheritance; Voltore is happy to take advantage of the delicate republican legal system from which he gets his sustenance and identity. All three are made gullible by their own vanity and greed. But avarice as a folly so often leads to premeditation, even to vicious and cold-blooded crime, that Jonson must be especially careful of its humorous value. And he is.

In this chapter, I would like to show how precisely Shakespeare has expropriated Jonson's form and how he has injected into it a criticism of the morality of Jonson's gull-catching satire. To do so, I must "exorcize"—as Toby's final maneuver exorcizes Malvolio—the downstairs plot, remove it and study it in isolation, quite unreasonably, because the two plots are, as I will show, ultimately fused "at the hip." In the downstairs "Jonsonian" comedy of *Twelfth Night*, Shakespeare makes Sir Toby Belch's butt a more thoroughly passionate dupe than Jonson's. His designed traps certainly play on the vanity of material acquisitiveness, especially in conjunction with love matters, but Shakespeare's sequence of confidence games requires only that each victimized gull suffer from affectation of one's appeal for the female sex and one's martial capacities, that is, would-be "machismo." The audience inevitably sides with an exposure of the most ludicrous folly of affected valor and irresistability, a bias intensified for the original audience by a strong sense of the downstairs plot's contemporaneity. In good Jonsonian practice, to effect an "Image of the day," Shakespeare has reminded his audience of popular songs like "There dwelt a man in Babylon," Brownist, Puritan and other sectarian and religious controversies, new maps of the Americas, visits to the Shah, of imprisonment for demon-possession, supposed real or fake exorcism, new sweet wines from the Canary Islands, enthusiasm for astrology and pseudomedicine, new five-step dances from France, recent Arctic voyages, wonderful oversized beds from Ware, newly recognized symptoms of venereal disease, strictures on dueling, and most notably, bear-baiting, a reference that draws the audience ominously into the environs of the Globe Theatre in Bankside itself.

Like Volpone's, Toby's first con game is already in operation when the play opens. As the drama moves downstairs (1.3), so to speak, from the seacoast of Illyria, into the realm of citizen comedy. Aguecheek, whose name in part suggests the face rash of the sanguine personality, is being led to believe that he has an excellent chance of winning the hand of Toby's niece, the countess Olivia, thus gaining the advantages of her estate. In return for the contrived perpetuation of his "vain" wish, Andrew buys all drink, food, and entertainment, no doubt the canary wine, pickled herring, and bear-baiting enjoyed by Toby and his cohorts. Maria says to Toby that she has heard Olivia talk

> of a foolish knight that you brought in one night here to be her wooer.
> *Toby.* Who? Sir Andrew Aguecheek?
> *Maria.* Ay, he.
> *Toby.* He's as tall a man as any's in Illyria.
> *Maria.* What's that to th' purpose?
> *Toby.* Why, he has three thousand ducats a year.
> *Maria.* Ay, but he'll have but a year in all these ducats. (1.3.14–21)

I suppose Maria means in this interchange that the very source of Andrew's yearly income will dry up in an extravagant twelve months with conning Toby.

A "morally" acceptable cony (rabbit) or gull, Andrew also suffers delusions of sexual appeal that suit the opposite aspect of his "would-be" machismo, described by Maria,

> and but that he hath the gift of a coward to allay the gust he hath in quarrelling, 'tis thought among the prudent he would quickly have the gift of a grave. (1.3.27–30)

Andrew's fear may have saved his affected valor from a test in the past, but not in the near future. During the conning of Andrew, the audience remains strongly with *parasitus* Toby until, I think, his very last words, when—Olivia married—Toby in a fit of mad injured rage calls Andrew "an ass-head and a coxcomb and a knave, a thin-faced knave, a gull" (5.1.198). A macho gull Andrew is, and one must applaud his very "moral" punishment. His education should cost. After all, he lived in the deluded hope that the incipient bonds with Olivia and enjoyment of her estate would defray all his costs. But I think Andrew ultimately gains some sympathy through Toby's harsh condemnation. As shall be seen, bias in favor of Toby and his plots must "slip" toward the conclusion of the "downstairs," citizen plot. As in the more severe case of Volpone, in the end one can no longer delight unambiguously in Toby's triumphs.

Cony-catching plot number two—featuring Maria's forged letter—victimizes the house steward Malvolio for his would-be machismo regarding his pretense of irresistability but also his urge to lord it over the household. Generally speaking, Maria suggests him into a state of excitation, but he does remember Olivia herself saying "that, should she fancy, it should be one of my complexion" (2.5.23–24). I suppose that Olivia said that because she was in deep mourning for her brother, and rejecting the Duke Orsino, she would not fall in love except with a dour and phlegmatic fellow like Malvolio—Mr. Ill-wish—that is, she would neither love nor marry, as heard elsewhere. But Malvolio's regard for his manly sex appeal keeps him from finding Olivia's true feelings. At the height of his vain fit, when, as Fabian remarks, "imagination blows him" (2.5.39), he dreams out loud of calling Toby to him,

> having come from a day-bed, where I have left Olivia sleeping. (2.5.45–46)

Here he no doubt imagines violent love making to have produced an exhausted and somnolent Olivia while he wanders through his new house to imperial purpose. To the delight of Shakespeare's contemporary audience, Malvolio's vanity surprises the traditional classical and Renaissance idea that men are put to sleep by such exertion, women wakened. Thus Malvolio outdoes the Mars of Renaissance painting,[15] and is met by Toby's aside, "Fire and brimstone!" If he did not consider himself such a notable sex object, he would perhaps have questioned the need to emphasize the shape of his legs in yellow stockings cross-gartered and would have been more cautious in his final advance on Olivia, which leads to appropriate imprisonment and mock exorcism:

Olivia. Wilt thou go to bed, Malvolio?
Malvolio. To bed? Ay, sweetheart, and I'll come to thee. (3.4.27–28)

Is he listening? Partly, but mostly he is dreaming the dreams of affected machismo. The dark room of his commitment suits his blindness toward Olivia, as the mock exorcism suits his would-be "puritanic" severity. Malvolio's sickness "of self-love" (1.5.85) makes the audience desire such entrapment.

Con game number three, culminating in the set-up duel between Viola dressed as Cesario and Andrew, I argue, remains in keeping with the morally correct Jonsonian citizen comedy, although some productions of the play partially obscure this "generic probability" and leave the audience in an odd confusion. Sir Andrew Aguecheek's false bravado, as I have shown, is fair game, but how could a so often frail and very female Viola be suffering from delusions of machismo? And how could the audience be made to side with her tormentors? I suggest that the "star system," born, largely, of eighteenth-century stage practice, allowing for "leading ladies" to acquire this brilliant role, too often helps install an "unmanly" Viola in the play's leading role. Surely Viola must present a true likeness of her rather male brother, Sebastian, or the audience will have to assume that all other characters in the play are mad when, on the stage, they mistake Sebastian for his twin.[16] Viola adopts and enjoys a convincingly masculine disguise in the process of somehow "becoming" her supposed dead brother. Thus she swaggers and storms through Olivia's gate, and when she meets with Maria and the Countess, she employs contemptuous overfamiliarity and other forms of heroic sarcasm that go far with Olivia's supposedly hardened sexual sensibility.

Seeing the ladies ready to smile, for example, Cesario warns,

> Good beauties, let me sustain no scorn. I am very comptible, even to the least sinister usage. (1.5.166–68)

The possibility that she may be "comptible," vengeful and thoroughly accountable, in maintaining her honor, with her strength, as well as, perhaps, the sword at her side, is not lost on the ladies, and they alter their behavior. When she describes her version of manly wooing, is she not thoroughly out of Viola's part, and even the Duke's messenger's part—out of her "commission" entirely—and into Cesario's own part? She would

> Cry out 'Olivia!' O, you should not rest
> Between the elements of air and earth
> But you should pity me.
>
> (1.5.260–62)

This male ardor wins a typically Shakespearean female "come-on" from Olivia: "You might do much." Viola/Cesario is not overplaying her part for purposes of concealment. She is affected, and in a thoroughly warm-blooded way. The arranged duel punishes her for liking too well her macho and very real inflaming of Olivia and her swaggering—combined, of course, with that deep reluctance to use the sword at her side. Ultimately, she is reduced in this violent man's world to the aside.

> Pray God defend me! A little thing would make me tell them how much I lack of a man. (3.4.282–83)

Somewhat irrationally, that little thing suggests the male sexual organ, which should go with that hated sword, as it does metaphorically in the play.[17] In a savage world where survival depends on martial ability, that sword is as fun to wear and unfun to use, for her, as for Andrew. Like Andrew, Viola suffers a delusion brought on by vanity. Only such a would-be macho Viola could ever make a civilized audience laugh with Toby and Fabian at her terrible trepidation.

Ben Jonson scrupulously worried that the ending of *Volpone* would seem to his audience a breaking of generic convention. His unjoyful denouement, with Mosca sentenced to be a "perpetual prisoner in our gallies" and Volpone to lie in prison "crampt with irons," although, as Jonson says "not without some lines of example, drawne even from the ancients themselves,"[18] was a "liberty" whose "speciall ayme" was "to put the snaffle [bridle bit] in their mouths, that crie out, we never punish vice in our enterludes." As I have suggested, I believe that the audience expects such an ending as a result of the near rape of Celia, who, although she is treated as a possession by Voltore, by her own lack of greed is a pawn and not entirely fair game for Volpone's cony-catching. Here sexual attraction has caught the master cony-catcher at his own game. But is Toby's punishment not also, in a sense, directly related to sexual machinations?

Although he is drunk, naturally, when he is last seen, wounded and in need of "Dick Surgeon," Toby's relatively joyful punishment has just come in the form of the yoke of marriage to Maria. The play is full of omens about marriage between the wild, hard-drinking Toby and Maria. Feste, in his first appearance in act 1, says to Maria, "Many a good hanging prevents a bad marriage" (1.5.18), and "If Sir Toby would leave drinking, thou wert as witty a piece of Eve's flesh as any in Illyria" (1.5.24). These omens, however, are not tragic, but comic, especially in Toby's promise to marry Maria for her part in the gulling of Malvolio. They merely point to the role that he must give up, that of the reckless and "untamed" male. Thus in the final song, Feste tells all, "But when I came, alas, to wive . . . By swaggering could I never thrive" (5.1.386–388). Shakespeare has ingeniously designed Toby's punishment in the form of Viola's and Orsino's and Olivia's and Sebastian's reward, marriage. The citizen comedy's chastening thus borrows the form of the romance's expected reward. Jonsonian comedy and "hated" romance merge. The denouement of Shakespeare's citizen comedy provides both punishment and joy. Toby must simply move on from his last role to his next, lest

>'Gainst knaves and thieves men shut their gate,
>
>(5.1.384)

as Olivia might otherwise do when she says, raging over Sebastian's danger, that Toby is "Fit for the mountains and the barbarous caves" (4.1.44). The carefully orchestrated emotional effect of "laughing" with Toby at his sporting "with humane follies" successfully leads ultimately to the audience's laughing with and at his own comeuppance, his marriage to Maria. This laughter at the groom's "getting caught" is part of any real or mythic marriage ceremony. Shakespeare, however, will not allow imputation of the special "morality" of Jonson's kind of comedy to pass. Thus, I argue, he leaves his audience in the ambiguous state of laughing at an announced scapegoat.

One notable image in this play, that very contemporary one for Shakespeare's audience with its referent so dreadfully close to the play, shared by "upstairs" and "downstairs," is bear baiting. "Downstairs," to Fabian's remark that Malvolio brought him "out o'favor with my lady about a bear-baiting here" (2.5.7), Toby says significantly, "To anger him we'll have the bear again, and we will fool him black and blue." It looks, in fact, as if the bear is to be Malvolio himself. On the other hand, "upstairs," Olivia, thinking about the terrible risk to her own very feminine sense of decency in sending the ring after Viola/Cesario, allows that image to expand suddenly into a much larger "ring." Thus she scolds Viola/Cesario:

> Have you not set mine honor at the stake
> And baited it with all th'unmuzzled thoughts
> That tyrannous heart can think?
> (3.1.115–17)

Of course, Viola/Cesario has baited Olivia with her so masculine and threatening words, and Olivia must learn in the final scene that she was—like Malvolio by Feste/Topas—a gull of disguise. This cruel image of the staked bear ominously controls the play upstairs and downstairs, and suggests a gentle criticism of Jonson's kind of plot, because, as perfect as it is,[19] it requires the audience's collective emotions to gang up, if with "poetic justice" on its side, on a victim, one of whom jars the audience by storming off the stage of *Twelfth Night* at its close. When Malvolio complains of having been "made the most notorious geck and gull / That e'er invention played on" (5.1.333–34), the audience must recognize its own collusion in victimizing not only a person made gullible by his own conceit, but a "geck," a "natural," not an "affected" focus of its scorn. Clearly, Jonsonian "invention" has its cruel side, and Shakespeare has indirectly adominished its audience for spite. Furthermore, Shakespeare has proven in this play that he could take Jonson's kind of plot and successfully unify it with the kind of fabulous story or myth that Jonson decried and Aristotle considered accidental to the true worth of a drama.[20]

Competition in this war of words and ideologies between

Shakespeare and Jonson serves to clarify the identities of the participants and generates new distinctions, as I have shown, in the case of Jonson's new dramatic form and Shakespeare's composite masterpiece. Unlike mimetic rivalry, such announced competition promotes new combinations rather than squelching all originality in mimetic response. The fecundity of public controversy, however, can, as I shall show in the following chapter, yield to critical victimization, especially when texts survive their creators, above all, when they "publish" the evils of the sacrificial process they are about to undergo.

8

Sacrificing the Mysteries: Dismembering the Text in Early Criticism of Shakespeare's *Julius Caesar*

In *Julius Caesar*, as I have suggested, Shakespeare examines steps of a process observed in human affairs from the microcosm of disorder in the schoolyard to the macrocosm of international strife. In all political situations one likes to see healthy competition but often witnesses an awful scrambling. To borrow Cassius's words,[1] a step toward disintegration might occur when "things change from their ordinance" (1.3.66), creating an absence of "quality and kind" (1.3.64), when political and social identity is leveled out thanks to flattery and self-flattery at the top and ensuing uncertainty within a hierarchy. Fundamental distinctions between people and their roles no longer exist: "Old men, fools, and children calculate" (1.3.65). In step two, rivalry reigns in the vacuum of power. Where rank is literally devalued, one retains one's honor "by reflection" (1.2.68). The rival does not know who he is because he is unconsciously engaged in imitation, a game of reflexive daring, "with hearts of controversy" (1.2.109) not reflection. This political chaos is beyond human control—"heaven hath infused them with these spirits / To make them instruments of fear and warning" (1.3.69–70). And it spreads.

In step three, however, an unchecked disaster of envy and emulation may be contained and unity restored in concentrating all energy on a victim—often the flattered ruler himself—but if his destruction is too self-conscious or not unanimous, that victim's "falling sickness" (1.2.254) may itself be caught by the sacrificers. To "stoop then and wash" (3.1.111) in his blood, even to consider the ritual of "this our lofty scene . . . acted over" (3.1.112) may only cause the violence to flare up again. The victim will not "now become a god" (1.2.115) as befits such sacrificial ritual, and his blood will prove to be the opposite of life-giving: in fact, bad blood. Furthermore, in their desperate avoidance of what is "womanish" (1.3.84), the conspirators will appear to the mass of people to be subhuman. Cassius's own warning that Romans are "sheep," "hinds," "offal," "trash," "rubbish" (1.3.105 ff.) will come true in relation to his own plot in renewed violence.

After all, Cassius has already pointed out that the elements of the mob or clique or conspiracy are not really human but metaphoric things as insignificant as kindling: "those that with haste will make a mighty fire / Begin it with weak straws" (1.3.107–108). Shakespearean tragedy dwells on that sad moment of human existence when man behaves not unlike wolves and other pack animals. Tragedy tends to present political situations where, as opposed to enjoying the differentiating light of Apollonian comedy—when humans are capable of reason, of speech, political animals, above all animals capable of laughter—humans remain in Dionysian darkness when the savage in them is dreadfully near, when they are little more than imitative animals, mere working cogs in a process of political decline.

Comedy leads to the unifying ritual of marriage, tragedy to funeral where unity must be too carefully preserved. Thanks to its liturgical origins, tragedy seems likely to expose this fatal process. After all, Greek tragedy tends to provide versions of the events leading up to Dionysian dismemberment and resurrection, as Christian tragedy in its original form of passion, miracle, or mystery play, develops versions of the events leading to Calvary. In this context, Pentheus and Adam always suggest types of Dionysus and Christ. But much tragedy does not openly criticize misuse of that sacred process, as Shakespeare does on several occasions. Such open analysis of such mysteries can cause offense, and, as in the case of *Julius Caesar* and the English neoclassical tradition, response to the offense may take the form of bringing the sacrificial process to the text itself.

In the age that encompasses the appearance of Ben Jonson's *Sejanus* in 1603 to that of Samuel Johnson's *Irene* in 1749, overt reference to religious mysteries in tragedy tends to disappear.[2] Dramatic concentration on historical events per se and ensuing tension between love and honor in the minds of tragic protagonists unfolds a political and psychological "play-world" apart from the sacred and supernatural. On political and religious grounds—above all, on "rational grounds"—reenacting tragedy's primitive origins was taken to be an error in decorum. The notion of removal of society's victim and that of providential ending—what Thomas Rymer called "poetic justice"—for example, came in conflict, and the latter held sway, most notably perhaps in Nahum Tate's "revised" ending of *Lear*. Placing *Julius Caesar* in the climactic position of what was otherwise a chronological list of Shakespeare's four major tragedies, John Dennis rues the absence of poetic justice in "the *Hamlet*, the *Othello*, the *Mackbeth*, the *King Lear*, or the *Julius Caesar* in all which the good and bad perish promiscuously."[3] A new kind of tragedy—and a new way of looking at tragedy—replaces the old of Marlowe, Shakespeare, and Webster. As Eric Rothstein has said, "Restoration tragic theory developed, like Restoration tragedy, by subverting the tradition on which it drew."[4] A play whose words and images evoke the sacrificial process, like Shakespeare's *Julius Caesar*, becomes painfully visible, and it must be altered. But a dismembered text must be "re-membered," or some of its implications will be permanently set aside.

The first known calls for removal or alteration of elements of the play antedate the appearance of the folio and, I believe, ultimately concern Ben Jonson's uneasiness with Shakespeare's sacrificial theme, although they also manifest the competition between warring playwrights discussed in chapter 7. Jonson's criticism and mimicry of Shakespeare's words in *Julius Caesar*, in part, shows resentment that "natural"[5] Shakespeare, supposedly of limited knowledge of the ancients, chose a subject so central to an understanding of the "golden age" of Latin in late Republican Rome. In the mythos of their rivalry, Shakespeare is sometimes seen retorting to Jonson's supposed slurs on his "smale Latin" by suggesting that Jonson was a translator from the Latin, not a poet. Nicholas L'Estrange tells of an elaborate "Shakespearean" quibble on the word *latten* (Latin, "brass") delivered on the occasion of standing as godfather to one of Ben Jonson's children: "I'le e'en give him a douzen good Lattin spoones, and thou shalt translate them."[6] Aside from suggesting that Jonson would melt down ("translate") his child's spoons in miserly fashion, this jest would serve to remind Jonson of his remarkably close use of Tacitus and Suetonius and others in his Roman tragedies, *Catiline*, and especially the excellent but ill-received *Sejanus*, in which Shakespeare played, perhaps as the emperor Tiberius.

Over a century later, however, Samuel Johnson would complain that *Julius Caesar* was "somewhat cold and unaffecting"[7] precisely because Shakespeare himself, like Jonson, purportedly, rendered too closely his classical sources, presumably Plutarch (though the play contains hints of Cicero, Suetonius, and others).[8] Therefore, it is not surprising to hear that "in Plume's version of the latten spoon anecdote, the roles are reversed."[9] What such a mythos suggests is that Shakespeare and Jonson were rivals accusing each other of similar things that they were both performing, but they were also aware of the procedure, and their plays openly show and thus "criticize" characters submerging their identities—or becoming virtually identical—in rivalry over goals that slowly begin to disappear. In Shakespeare the initial goal is more often a sexual one—witness, for example, Hortensio, a young man, and Gremio, an old man, merging identities in a struggle at least initially over Bianca's love in *Taming of the Shrew*, though she is spurned by both "lovers" in a moment. In Jonson, the disappearing goal is usually the power that comes with wealth—witness the fatal rivalry in *Volpone* between Mosca and Volpone, whose goal was initially money, but that money comes to mean everything and nothing in the play. Jonson's criticism of *Julius Caesar*, I argue, however, also reflects genuine neoclassical uneasiness with Shakespeare's "sacrificial" theme that led to dangerous "critical" consequences.

Ben Jonson seems to have brought about the change of a line in the folio version, which he claimed was "ridiculous":[10]

> Caesar never did wrong but with just cause.

Jonson probably considered it impossible for the great Latin rhetorician and prose master, the "golden" Julius Caesar, to utter such a paradox, and the remark was apparently exchanged for the retort,

> Know, Caesar doth not wrong, nor without cause
> Will he be satisfied.
> (3.1.47–48)

The deleted remark,[11] however, seems more consistent to this reader with the Caesar of Shakespeare's play, a man made most visible by his godlike confidence in ends justifying means, as he moves, in the face of all signs and omens, toward his own death. His irrational contempt for danger as well as his susceptibility to Decius Brutus's flattering prediction that he is ordained to prove a fountain for the populace from which "great Rome shall suck / Reviving blood" (2.2.87–88), recall Calphurnia's remark that his "wisdom is consumed in confidence" (2.2.49). Here, he is merely asserting that he lives beyond the human law of right and wrong, that the ruler must rightly wrong on occasion. The picture of Caesar congratulating himself on his judicious use of "wrong"—"harm" as well as "evil"—at the instant of his destruction at the swords of the ring of conspirators is a terrifying spectacle reminiscent of the Theban tyrants, Oedipus or Pentheus, immediately before their catastrophic falls. His "divine" madness and hubris are not reasonable.

Jonson, however, seems not only to have been offended by the "irrationality" of Shakespeare's would-be sacrificial victim, Caesar, but also by the presentation of the member of a group of men—be it aristocratic conspiracy or citizenry—as lacking reason at the moment of their destruction of the would-be *pharmakos*. In *Every Man Out of His Humour* (5.6.79), he scoffs at Shakespeare's latinized version of Caesar's Greek remark to Brutus in Suetonius's *De Vita Caesarum*, "Et Tu, Brutè" (3.1.77). Paralleling English and Latin to Latin and Greek, however, seems perfectly apt. Intimacy with Brutus is suggested by Caesar's reserving a "foreign" tongue for his friend. As I have argued, Shakespeare is removing ("and you, child [or son]") any hint that Caesar may be Brutus's father, but of course the playwright who Samuel Johnson said would gladly give up the world for a "quibble" could not resist a reference to the unmanly "brutality" of Brutus at this moment. This idea, that men shift into metaphoric "brutes" when they act unanimously, seems to have bothered Jonson, perhaps here, but certainly elsewhere. Again in *Every Man Out* (3.4.33), he parodies Mark Antony's remark "O judgement, thou art fled to brutish beasts, / And men have lost their reason" (3.2.104–105), ostensibly because it contradicts the Aristotelian doctrine that man is uniquely capable of reason.[12]

Shakespeare's *Julius Caesar*, however, as I have argued, dwells on man's tendency to commit unhuman or subrational group murder when individual social identity is lost in uniform disguise. A group is not rational in its violence, and neither is its victim in his half-conscious move to his own destruction. Jonson may well be expressing his uneasiness with the investigation of that most "irrational" of religious mysteries, sacrifice, but he is engaging in the process as a critic of Shakespeare's text. When *Julius Caesar* came to Jonson's mind, as he wrote *Timber: or Discoveries Made upon Men and Matters*, he was contemplating Shakespeare's failure to remove "a thousand" lines, and his language suggests a call to sacrifice portions of the text: "Blotted out," "blotted," "stop'd," "*Sufflaminandus erat*" ("he had to be repressed in speaking"), "before wee sow our land, we should plough it."[13] Lines in the play seemed defective, and fit for removal, and the leading critics of the neoclassical age Jonson helped usher in concurred. But what they earmarked for removal was exposure of the sacrificial process they were in fact reenacting.

Thomas Rymer, severe in his attack on Shakespeare's supposed affront to the Roman nobility in *A Short View of Tragedy* (1692), was especially aroused by a hint of such a savage spectacle as the ceremonial aftermath of human sacrifice in Caesar's death. He argues that realism or "history"[14] is upheld in Brutus's "noble" comments "Let's be sacrificers . . . Let's carve him as a dish fit for the gods" (2.1.166–73), but is contradicted in his exhortation to "bathe our hands in Caesar's blood / Up to the elbows" (3.1.106–7). Rymer bases his objection somewhat capriciously on an *ad hominem* argument that Shakespeare, supposedly a butcher and a butcher's son, is daring to characterize a Roman aristocrat as a butcher. Oddly in this circumstance, carving Caesar is acceptable but bathing in his blood is not. In the main source for the story of Shakespeare's low profession, John Aubrey remarks that when Shakespeare "kill'd a Calfe he would doe it in a high style, and make a Speech."[15] Whatever the truth of the anecdote, here is a parodic version of those conventional speeches proclaiming the immortality of the victim that Mark Antony presents over the corpses first of Julius Caesar then of Brutus. Is it possible that Rymer is attracted to the "butcher" theory because of Shakespeare's emphasis on sacrificial "carving" in this play? At any rate, some of Brutus's words and much else concerning this ominous tragic element in the play proved fit for removal.

T. Killigrew, around 1719, concluding that "Brutus is Certainly a deffecttive Charracter at best," gives some ground rules of emendation of the play "no more that a ruled paper, for others to write on."[16] notably excluding Brutus's "beautifully poetical" rationalization of the murder of Caesar because it "will Iustifie my killing any man,"[17] and also "Et tu Brutè—then fall Caesar." His plan is to blot out any suggestion that Caesar may invite pathos and that Brutus may seem "irrational" or "brutal" in the assassination. Killigrew's argument is apparently political—Brutus is republican and senatorial in contrast to Caesar's supposed monarchic bias—but without explicit justification, subtle reference in Shakespeare's play to the sacrificial mechanism is also being blurred, then excluded, in steps.

John Sheffield, duke of Buckingham, soon produces what he

calls an "alteration" of *Julius Caesar* in two parts, *The Tragedy of Julius Caesar* and *The Death of Marcus Brutus*, "not at all unlike what would result from an application of Killigrew's 'ruled paper.'"[18] The opening scene of face-off between tribunes and citizens in holiday garb is replaced by senatorial discussion of Caesar's tyranny, and when the tradesmen of Shakespeare's first scene finally appear, the impertinent jesting with the tribunes has disappeared with the tribunes themselves. The "holiday" or fertility ritual, the Lupercalia, is now Roman "sports," removing among other things the wry effect of Brutus's atheistic reference to this most venerable ritual as "games" (1.2.178).

Since Sheffield's play ends decorously with Mark Antony's funeral oration, the parallel dismemberment of Cinna the poet on the grounds of his first name (3.3), moreover, and the "round table" proscription scenes (4.1) are also set aside.[19] Now a villainous Cassius, not Brutus, calls to "bathe our hands in Caesar's blood," apparently in order to soil clothes to terrify the citizens, and Brutus objects on moral grounds[20] and abstains. The ceremonial wash now has its lowly reasons, rejected by the supremely rational Brutus. And the act is no longer unanimous among the conspirators. Not surprisingly, Sheffield's adaptation seems to have influenced his friend Alexander Pope's emendation of the play. Pope, in his edition of Shakespeare's play, though he states that he will religiously preserve the outstanding folio text,[21] transfers "Let us bathe our hands" to Casca without textual support.[22]

In Sheffield, the play has been "translated," carried over, into the neoclassical idiom, concentrating attention on entirely legitimate themes, such as the conflict of love and honor in Brutus, Stoical thought, and republican politics. Such adaptation, however, is more than a consistent application of principles of poetic justice and decorum and development of philosophical and political aspects of the play. There is also—in the guise of elimination of certain obvious flaws in Shakespeare's composition—exclusion of the "mysterious" theme of sacrifice itself, a theme, as many recent critics have noted,[23] that provides one key to understanding this disturbing play. I now move on to examine Shakespeare's versions of the contagion of political "dis-ease" in man's institutions and in his soul in the schematic pictures of oligarchy in *Much Ado about Nothing* and tyranny in *Macbeth*.

PART 4

Self-Destructive Tyranny in Oligarchy and Monarchy

9
England's Sicily and Shakespeare's Critique of Gallantry in *Much Ado about Nothing*

Today, any attempt to identify symbolically the two largest islands sitting on the edge of continental Europe, Sicily and England, might seem a remote enterprise. For example, would an image of the supposed home (for British eyes safely placed in the Mediterranean) of vigilante justice and internecine strife (that is, no policemen, or rather no effective policemen) apply to British life and to the British bobby? The very phrases, such as *vendetta, mafia, cosa nostra,* and to a lesser extent *la mano nera,* suggest political mechanisms remote to Shakespeare's or is it Gaunt's would-be "scept'red isle" (*Richard II* 2.1.40), ideally a most orderly "precious stone set in the silver sea" (46), or, indeed, any more recent concept of British rule or *Pax Britannicum?* But Shakespeare, I argue, equated the two on a pair of occasions to "schematize" the universality of the joys and horrors of patriarchal ways, and the unique problem of gallantry as an ideal.

Sicily and England traditionally shared some peculiar traditions and lineage. Tina Whitaker early pointed out that "the island was made a representative kingdom much about the same time as England, and by the same adventurous race that swept away the Anglo-Saxon dynasty."[1] The parliamentary tradition of Sicily that continues to this day created a perceived link between Palermo and London in the English medieval and Renaissance mind that remained more significant than parallel Norman rule, the countries' identical treasury systems—probably of Sicilian origin[2]—the bonds created by intermarriage of royalty, and the extended visits between rulers and dignitaries such as Richard Coeur de Lion and Thomas à Beckett to Sicily, and important expatriates such as Walter of England, archbishop of Palermo, primate and chancellor of Sicily, and translator of Aesop's fables.

In the later sixteenth century, after Venetian liberties were curtailed, the English and the Sicilians were proud to boast the only remaining effective constitutional parliaments in the world, both peculiar in that they ruled or nearly or barely ruled through the authority of perhaps the two leading sovereigns of Europe at emnity, Philip II of Spain and Elizabeth I of England. Maybe the tenuous disconnection of these "almost-peninsulas" by means of the Strait of Messina and the English Channel allowed for experimentation in more popular forms of government, where freedom or license, as the case may be, could, in some sense, be contained or quarantined.

Respecting Sicily's constitutional past, when Alfonso took over Sicily in the 15th century, the king of Aragon announced that "although united to Spain, she should retain her independence, her constitution, and a separate Parliament,"[3] and while that supposed independence from Spain was questionable, and the island nation was not a little exploited in the 16th century to support Spanish imperial adventures, notably in the New World, it is clear that she received special treatment among Spain's imperial lands. The historian Helmut Koenigsberger points out that it was popularly thought of Spanish hegemony specifically in Italy that "in Sicily the Spaniards nibbled, in Naples they ate, and in Milan they devoured."[4]

Koenigsberger goes on to mention that central basis for emotional identity of the two islands: "In the early seventeenth century Sicilians claimed that only two Parliaments still preserved their rights and powers: London and Palermo." Thus, for example, when Shakespeare's constable Dogberry and his inferiors, Hugh Oatcake and George Seacoal, show up in the streets of Messina, the audience is not simply baffled by anachronism, but asked to look at a version of English municipal police,[5] but in a city and an island that apparently has always inherited symbolic meaning, for Shakespeare and others, as the locale of male-oriented society where admiration for military virtues and a strained sense of honor prevails. Sicily's mythos of honor,[6] especially regarding female chastity and decorum, in the popular mind, enjoins duels and other forms of reciprocal violence likely to break down civic order and due process. Indeed, its very tradition of self-determination, as in the myth of the Old West, may seem to encourage the development of such a "social order." I argue that Shakespeare, in part, provides a critique of machismo and rivalry over women and other possessions in a patriarchal society in both his plays largely about Messina, Sicily, *Much Ado about Nothing* and *Winter's Tale*, but such an impetus to breakdown of civic order reflects events nearer home in England. Symbols are always metaphoric, yoking the imported with the local, the vehicle with the tenor, in this case, Sicily with Shakespeare's England.

Koenigsberger, in his analysis of the function of the Parliament of Palermo in the sixteenth century, convincingly argues that by means of the existence of the viceroy in Palermo, Philip II relieved himself of direct Sicilian criticism by allowing all blame for policy-making to focus on the viceroy himself. Koenigsberger's culminating argument concerns Marc Antonio Colonna, viceroy to Sicily from 1577 to 1584, and the notorious pan-European scandal that surrounded the final events of his substitute reign and his recall and questionable death in Spain in 1584. The evidence shows a peculiar Sicilian feud of jealousy, murder, and revenge that results in part from the breakdown of formal restraint in society, in part from universal problems in patriarchal societies. Dangerously sifting through accusations and counteraccusations, and other biased accounts, and following Koenigsberger's scholarly reconstruction of events, I discover the following probable facts.

In Palermo in the early 1580s lives a rich, probably thoroughly chaste and "honorable," curiously forceful, though silent, young and beautiful woman, Eufrosina Zaragossa, wife to a young profligate, Galceran Corbera, who, however, remains under his father's patriarchal, even more spendthrift, control. When Galceran's wife, Eufrosina, refuses to defray debts her father-in-law, baron of Miserandino, has amassed, the patriarch apparently convinces his son—exactly how is not known—that his wife is having an affair with her page. He arranges for the torture of this page, and when the boy refuses to implicate the baroness, the baron murders him. Now the viceroy, Marc Antonio Colonna, the would-be policeman but inevitable target for victimization in the tradition of vulnerable Madrid-appointed Viceroys, intervenes. He administratively banishes the father-in-law, Miserandino, although on the advice of the president of the Great Court, the highest ranking native in the country's parliamentary system, the murder of the page is covered up.

Now popularly rumored to be the lover of Eufrosina Zaragossa, the Viceroy Colonna himself becomes the center of attention in a vendetta that eventually claims, or probably claims, the lives of all principals. The father, Miserandino, collapses and dies in debtor's prison, rumored to be poisoned. The son receives multiple knife wounds, possibly by hire, probably by adventurer friends of a prostitute Galceran has been visiting, and is left dead in the streets of Malta. Eufrosina Zaragossa remarries and is strangled by her new stepsons in Rome, who apparently resent the supposed fact that her father married another man's mistress.

Marc Antonio Colonna, of course, has convincingly portrayed Eufrosina to Philip II as a chaste wife, and he claims that whenever she is with him she is constantly chaperoned by one of Palermo's most respected ladies, a claim that was easily verified, but Colonna's enemies take that argument itself as a confession of sorts. The sons of Eufrosina's new husband in Rome pay with their lives. Finally the only survivor among the principles, the Viceroy Colonna himself, when he is recalled to Spain in 1584, "Officially with full honours,"[7] by Philip II, dies of a fall, under mysterious circumstances, of an injury to his head, a concussion, on 1 August 1584, on his way to the court in Madrid.

Although Marc Antonio Colonna's death may well have resulted from natural causes, there are, inevitably, rumors of poison. One could claim that this "Websterian tragedy,"[8] as Koenigsberger calls it, is typical of Italy at large or even of the Spain of this period, but because it originates on Sicilian soil, and radiates out from there to the world at large, to Malta, Rome, Madrid, and so on, it became most resonant in the Europe of Shakespeare's day.[9] The fact that the odd parliamentary situation in Sicily may have helped bring about the rebirth of patriarchal custom ensured its notoriety in England. In the popular mind, Sicily seems always to have been the symbolic location of a patriarchal system, for good or for bad, in some magical, romantic, or symbolic sense. Shakespeare, I believe, makes use of that myth of Sicily, in *Much Ado about Nothing*, as he made use of the tradition of Ephesus as a land of white magic in *Comedy of Errors* or of Cyprus as the ancient eastern Mediterranean home of erotic love, thanks to its propinquity to Aphrodite's birthplace, in *Othello*.

As when he later presents Messina, Sicily, in a departure from Robert Greene, with a court dominated by a too jealously honorable and rigorous, aging lion, Leontes, in *Winter's Tale*, in *Much Ado about Nothing*, Shakespeare opens his play with the introduction of the governor of Messina, Leonato (another lion), liberal, sententious, and careful of the honor of his court in preparation for the arrival of Prince Pedro of Aragon. As the play progresses, one sees in Leonato all the virtues and faults of his patriarchal ways. Leonato's generosity seems unbounded, but perhaps somewhat beyond his means. Pedro's first words are:

Good Signior Leonato, you are come to meet your trouble? The fashion of the world is to avoid cost, and you encounter it. (1.1.85)

The visit seems casual, but the provisions are magnificent. Yet when banter leads to the silent presence of his daughter, Hero, in this men's society, Leonato affirms her legitimacy in an oblique manner, reflecting, perhaps, his uneasiness at maintaining honor in a world where women are, in a sense, sentient possessions, unstable repositories of one's reputation.

Thus, when Pedro reminds him again of his generosity, "You embrace your charge too willingly. I think this is your daughter," Leonato returns, "Her mother hath many times told me so" (1.1.92). This comment licences further banter:

Benedick. Were you in doubt, sir, that you asked her?
Leonato. Signor Benedick, no; for then were you a child.

Not to underestimate the good humor of these remarks, familiar ones in Shakespeare, one discovers that Leonato becomes, towards the close of the play, the man who tragically overreacts to his supposed loss of honor in his daughter, Hero.

Without deliberation, Leonato accepts through unreliable witnesses the story of Hero making love to Borachio at her window. And in so doing, he dwells on his own loss of honor in his daughter's blood. He rues the fact that if his daughter Hero had been an illegitimate orphan,

> 'This shame derives itself from unknown loins'?
> But mine, and mine I loved, and mine I praised,
> And mine that I was proud on—mine so much
> That I myself was to myself not mine.
> (4.1.133–36)

This strained wordplay, so often heard from Shakespeare's most distraught individuals, here, I believe, based on the several meanings of "mine," the first person possessive and an excavation for ore, underscores the notion that women in a patriarchal society are owned prizes—belonging to me (mine) and pits of earthly treasures (mines)—and like the military hardware they outvalue, they can easily be a source of dishonor that is total for the possessor.

> Valuing of her—why she, O, she is fall'n
> Into a pit of ink, that the wide sea

> Hath drops too few to wash her clean again,
> And salt too little which may season give
> To her foul tainted flesh!
>
> (4.1.137–41)

Once a mine of great value Hero has now magically fallen into a pit of ink, and her stains have become indelible. Because of such potential devaluation of women, the patriarch, Leonato, remains over-sensitive to his daughter's imminent fall from a state of honor, and now mere suspicion or unconfirmed rumor can cause a lethal overreaction. Hero, no doubt having been taught to keep quiet, except with other women, or, perhaps, with men behind the defilade of a mask, is ultimately condemned to dishonor by her father, in his men's world, for the ironic cause: "She not denies it" (4.1.171).

Among the great mass of male-oriented banter—needling, notably concerning women's infidelity and their likelihood, if one gets too close, of inflicting on men venereal disease and cuckoldry—and male-oriented activity—practical jokes designed for gulling, substitute wooing, and sabre-rattling of various sorts, sometimes dangerously involving old men like Leonato and Antonio—Beatrice, the notably unsilent woman, serves as the exception who proves the rule. An extraordinary female in this patriarchal society, she endorses its most rigorous concepts of honor, and I think Shakespeare forces us to question some of her behavior on these grounds. This heroine in her liberated and delightful banter about and with Benedick in the first scene of the play manages to question all aspects of his manhood, but to glorify a true manhood that is not a little violent and certainly uncontained and martial in combat and vendetta.

Before Benedick shows up on stage, Beatrice says that he is a feeble soldier yet a womanizer, challenging only "Cupid at the flight" (1.1.35). He is a liar and a coward:

> I pray you, how many hath he killed and eaten in these wars? But how many hath he killed? For indeed I promised to eat all of his killing. (1.1.37–39)

He is "a good soldier to a lady" (1.1.47). He is as witty as a horse. He is overlavish in his affections, yet unsteady, promiscuous in friendships.

> He hath every month a new sworn brother. (1.1.63)

The manly code of friendship and support for comrades in arms means little to him.

Benedick finally arrives on stage and, after unloosing some salvos of his own, appears to avoid Beatrice's verbal darts. She takes up the horse image again to suggest he suffers from cosmic impotence.

> You always end with a jade's trick. I know you of old. (1.1.129–30)

He ever slows down at the race's close. If having known Benedick "of old" suggests an earlier love-affair[10] and very female vulnerability, nevertheless, Beatrice fits in so well with all this "machismo" banter precisely because she supports its dangerous values. The cannibal metaphor she introduced in the early moment when she claimed she will eat all Benedick's killing, reappears in her central speech in the play, precisely because she would have men more manly, even more than they are—and if they are not manly enough she will eat them. Thus, I argue, Shakespeare shows us Beatrice reinforcing the male-oriented gallantry in the play. She announces that if men will not be men enough, as woman, she will be superman.

Fittingly, Beatrice gets to call for the "contract" on Claudio's life for having dishonored her cousin. She says to Benedick, "Kill Claudio" (4.1.285), and, as he hestitates and eventually transforms her request—as I read it—into a call for a challenge of Claudio to a duel, her refrain is heard:

> O that I were a man! . . . O God, that I were a man!
> I would eat his heart in the market-place.
> (4.1.298, 301–2)

Now Beatrice would metaphorically ritualize her vendetta in human sacrifice and ceremonial cannibalism. She would sacralize this very male proceeding.

Only the good English predecessor of the bobby, Constable Dogberry, can save society for another day from its incipient reciprocal violence revolving around the insulted maiden, and, if in a most exasperating and entertaining, bumbling yet perfect way, defuse the potential for violence in this Sicilian scene, turn Sicily back from bloodied almost peninsula of unpoliced mutual slaughter to "scept'red isle," that "fairest spot of the fruitful Earth," as Pindar puts it in his First Nemean Ode.

While Sicily, this much-maligned Mediterranean island, serves as a doubtful symbol for a universal political problem, an ancient Greek mythic location enjoying maddening beauty while it emblematizes, in the popular mind, a pan-Mediterranean location of male rivalry out of control, subjectively speaking, England is Sicily. The Sicily of the mind is merely what all societies would be when savage custom overwhelms due process, when human aggression creates a mobile political situation without proper arrests, without bobbies who can transform potential Websterian tragedy into Shakespearean tragicomedy, like Constable Dogberry and his force. As predetermined as such symbolic comparisons may appear, the shared heritage of self-determination of Sicily and England makes such coupling dramatically sound and particularly vibrant on the London stage. When civil war suddenly shook England after 1640, all easy distinctions may have dissolved.

10

What Rusts the Soul: Shakespeare's *Macbeth* and the Invention of the Conscience

One of the most compelling Renaissance traditions of rule in the state, of power, of proper government in the exterior domain of the prince, is, as I have suggested, the notion of necessary deception, indirection or hypocrisy, studied lie, needed covert violence, extenuated covert crime, a notion Machiavelli espoused for new rulers as did some of his conceptual progeny in England, such as Sidney, Greville, and Bacon. For the outside world, they recommend the behavior of the fox, not the lion.[1] Although such an earthbound and devious concept has always had Christian opponents, some of the most exciting thought about needed deception was developed in light of Christian theological bases and analogies, where the prince is pictured as a little god inscrutably ordering scourges and war for an unseen ulterior good, as God through the operation of nature may require rather than merely tolerate plague and flood and fire for purposes of purification. Of course, all this action points outward.

Man must live in his internal domain as well, as seen in Brutus's lonely words in the preface, sonnet 94's confession in chapter 1, and Henry V's soliloquy in chapter 3. While I examine several Shakespearean schemata of the positive effects of the dissimulating ruler in my early chapters, of Henry V in Great Britain, even, in the context of the family, the Petruchio of *Taming of the Shrew*, who sets up a school of hypocrisy, indirection, and tact for future members of polite society, Shakespeare does not allow one to overlook the internal damage brought about by dissembling. For example, while sonnet 94, by my reading, quite positively asks good rulers not to "do the thing they most do show" (l. 2), to be "the lords and owners of their faces" (l. 7), this poem also contains an eloquent warning about doing no "hurt"

(l. 1) and avoiding "base infection" (l. 11), which is largely internal.

Shakespeare, in fact, in precisely the period that he develops the soliloquy and the aside into the full-fledged internal monologue[2] begins to divulge the interior damage caused by personal dissimulation, deceit, and concealed crime. The fox's deception is now shown in *Hamlet, Othello,* and the so-called "problem plays" to rust the soul, even when the act of dissimulation may be healthy for the state at large. Souls deteriorate when their owners actively pretend, especially when other humans, notably friends, must die in their plans. Crimes without external punishment are strictly accounted for internally. For example, in *Macbeth,* even if Duncan is bleeding Scotland to death with his mercy and "meekness," thereby engendering civil war and foreign intervention before the play opens, his perhaps necessary, unavowed "assassination" (Macbeth's word) may cause infection in the new ruler. Macbeth's interior world may be susceptible to the terminal rust called "guilt."

Thanks, in part, I believe, to the influence of Michel de Montaigne's analysis of the internal damage brought by deception, Shakespeare, as he moved to high tragedy in the Jacobean era—with his sophisticated use of lonely words, especially ones overheard on the stage—presents in his theater an idea of the workings of conscience that the world, I believe, had never seen. Conscience, good or bad, once suggested mere consciousness of personal beneficence or ill that led to the delights in or worry about one's security or state of grace. The modern notion of gnawing conscience that cannot right certain wrongs the soul has commissioned, however, that kills off fundamental body functions, such as sleep and love-making, is, I believe, a concept of Montaigne staged in its entirety for the first time in Shakespeare's *Macbeth*. In a discussion of Macduff's purported "manly" valor, Eugene Waith remarks that "the development of Macbeth's character is a triumph of Lady Macbeth's ideal, for conscience, is stifled."[3] I argue, however, that as his outward crimes multiply, the drama of Macbeth's conscience merely moves inside. In monologue, Macbeth's inward consciousness shows a personal sense of dislocation from the universe by steps, notably in the disappearance of his soulmates, his comrades in arms and wife, and the eventual lack of a sense that the passage of time or the roles played in life including "King," have meaning.

Montaigne's most pointed discussion of the nature of the conscience, in his essay "Du Repentir," nicely translated by John

Florio as "Of Repenting"[4] to reflect Montaigne's notion of process, emphasizes the significance of the minutest passage of time in the maintenance of interior well-being. He insists on speaking of what he claims to be his own interior health, but he apparently means also to imply the opposite, the dis-eased and diseased soul. He initially claims he will not talk about the guilt one accumulates in the larger intervals of the stages of man's life, but rather in much narrower moments, because one's life, if well examined, continually and significantly alters itself:

> I describe not the essence, but the passage; not a passage from age to age, or as the people reckon, from seven years to seven, but from day to day, from minute to minute. (248)

The happiest state of man is the internal self-acceptance he calls a "good conscience" (250) that causes the mind to be

> Fraught with this self-joying delight and satisfaction.

He explains these good internal feelings, however, in terms of their opposites:

> It is no small pleasure for one to feel himself preserved from the contagion of an age so infected as ours, and to say to himself, "Could a man enter and see even into my soul, yet should he not find me guilty either of the affliction or ruin of anybody, not culpable of envy or revenge, nor of public offense against the laws, not tainted with innovation, trouble, or sedition, nor spotted with falsifying of my word." (250)

Macbeth, a publicly spotless man, suffers all those "guilts."

Montaigne later suggests that any bloody spot would actually color one's whole interior life. "It is not a spot but a dye that stains me" (256). And the color of the internal illness is blood red:

> Malice sucks up the greatest part of her own venom, and therewith empoisoneth herself. Vice leaveth, as an ulcer in the flesh, a repentence in the soul which still scratcheth and bloodieth itself. (249).

In *Hamlet*, one briefly heard this self-bloodying conscience speak in King Claudius's soliloquy, one narrowly not overhead by Hamlet:

> My stronger guilt defeats my strong intent,
> Like to a man to double business bound

> I stand in pause where I shall first begin,
> And both neglect. What if this cursèd hand
> Were thicker than itself with brother's blood,
> Is there not rain enough in the sweet heavens
> To wash it white as snow?
>
> (3.3.40–46)

Apparently, Hamlet, not hearing, only sees a kneeling gesture that deters him from separating by sword his uncle's seemingly contrite soul from his body. Claudio's speaking conscience, therefore, confirms the audience's suspicion of his guilt, but it does not enter the action of the play.

In *Macbeth*, however, one sees the career of the self-bloodying conscience develop into a central concern of the tragedy. Reflecting on his murder of a kinsman, a visitor to his house, and a king, Duncan, Macbeth asks, in a peculiar kind of soliloquy that is overheard, here, by Lady Macbeth,

> Will all great Neptune's ocean wash this blood
> Clean from my hand? No, this my hand will rather
> The multitudinous seas incarnadine
> Making the green one red.
>
> (2.2.59–62)

The image of unwashable, even odorous, blood on the hands reappears in the gestures and descriptions of Lady Macbeth in her sleepwalking scene (5.1). Macbeth's own central obsession, however, images blood simultaneously on the head of a victim and inside the head of the conscience-stricken perpetrator.

The workings of Macbeth's conscience, I feel, do not centrally concern his destruction of the king Duncan, who plausibly brought on, with his dangerous inaction, the near collaspe of his own kingdom, nor the gradual development of madness in his sometime overweening wife who, obsessed by Duncan's blood, apparently dies by suicide, but his murdering by proxy of his fellow in battle, his comrade in arms, Banquo. Such a "guilty" murder of Banquo produces Macbeth's gradual but total ruminative isolation and self-flagellation.

As in his pictures of Othello boldly narrating, not unlike *miles gloriosus*, to the Venetian senate, or ruminating violently in Desdemona's bedroom, Shakespeare dwells, in his "domestic" tragedy, *Macbeth*, on the Odyssean theme of the difficulty of the reintegration in civilized society of the professional warrior. The greatest joy of combat seems to be the closest sort of friendship, with a Cassio, or a Banquo, who in peacetime is easily alienated.

Battle's greatest horror is the constant fear of head injury, an image around which, I argue, Shakespeare schematizes his study of his warrior-king Macbeth's conscience.

One of the more exquisite debates in the history of Shakespeare criticism concerns the significance of the "naked new-born babe" (1.7.21) image of Macbeth's first soliloquy. Cleanth Brooks's presentation in *The Well Wrought Urn*,[5] Oscar James Campbell's answer,[6] and L. C. Knight's rebuttal[7] raise essential questions about Shakespeare's literary methods and intentions, partly because the apocalyptic baby appears in individual speeches but never on the stage. Therefore, it is virtually impossible to determine whether the image is idiosyncratic to the several speakers or of structural importance to the play as a whole. Not so with the head wound, which appears on stage and in speech, admirably emphasized in Roman Polansky's movie adaptation. The image of the bloodied head dominates the play by clear-cut authorial intention. This staged image should include Macbeth's head on a pike at the play's close and, I believe, also that of the "bloody" soldier at its opening.

In the second scene of the play a nonspecifically "bloody man" (1.2.1), the captain, relates how Macbeth and Banquo forcibly saved the kindgom from internal upheaval and invasion from the "Norweyan lord" (1.2.31)

> As cannons overcharged with double cracks,
> So they doubly redoubted strokes upon the foe.
> (1.2.37–38)

A picture of the fellowship of the two warriors alone on a highway after the battle follows. Shakespeare develops their relationship largely through the play of Banquo's sarcasm and Macbeth's laconic—sometimes ironic—response. What Banquo represents for Macbeth, for example, in the reiterate call to discuss the significance of the witches—an event that never happens—is friendship growing out of comradery in arms, yet Macbeth's envy of the supposed happy fate of Banquo's descendants comes between them, compelling his hired murder of his friend, killed in a flurry of head wounds.

King Duncan early says of Banquo,

> True, worthy Banquo: he is full so valiant,
> And in his commendations I am fed;
> It is a banquet to me.
> (1.4.54–56)

This wordplay on "Banquo" and "banquet" echoes in the play, for he is killed on the occasion of a festive dinner hypocritically designed for this "chief quest." Macbeth says, on the occasion of his dinner party,

> Let every man be master of his time
> Till seven at night. To make society
> The sweeter welcome, we will keep ourself
> Till supper time alone.
>
> (3.1.40–43)

Whether or not there is here a "papal we" referring only to Macbeth or to all "we," there is here a special savoring of "society" and good humor so essential to the sustenance of "good conscience" or humor. When, after Banquo has been treacherously dispatched, Macbeth calls for the party guests to

> sit down:
> At first and last the hearty welcome,
>
> (3.4.1–2)

internal disturbance causes Macbeth's feigned jocularity to take a startling turn that parallels the macabre humor of the scene of the Porter at the gate (2.3). When Banquo's murderer shows up—his head spotted with blood in such a way as to suggest Banquo's own—Macbeth points out "There's blood upon thy face" (3.4.14), as if such an unkempt visitor were inappropriate to a festive celebration of good fellowship. Yet the audience sees Macbeth's bloodied internal conscience in action, even in this odd call for propriety in his company. " 'Tis Banquo's then," the murderer replies. From this moment in the play, the bleeding head will suggest Macbeth's dislocation from the world at large—a drift into an internal bloodied conscience—that might have once included friends but never again. In the play, one ultimately hears Macbeth associate his own internal bloodied mind with that external bloodied head in a peculiar action of "conscience."

The murderer describes Banquo's corpse:

> Safe in a ditch he bides,
> With twenty trenchèd gashes on his head,
> The least a death to nature.
>
> (3.4.26–28)

To symbolize his farewell to friendship, Banquo's ghost appears to his treacherous friend with these head wounds and excludes

Macbeth from his not so mirthful table by taking his former comrade's seat. Macbeth at first addresses him directly,

> Never shake
> Thy gory locks at me.
> (3.4.50–51)

Macbeth sees the ghost asking him for repentence by this time-honored gesture of recrimination, and calls him on it from a strange kind of semiconsciousness.

This moment of confrontation, although the ghost remains invisible to the now alarmed guests, is thoroughly dramatic, but soon the audience drifts into the eery overheard soliloquy, a dramatic monologue directed at no one that reflects the voice of a jarringly "mirthful" or comic "conscience":

> The time has been
> That, when the brains were out, the man would die,
> And there an end. But now they rise again,
> With twenty mortal murders on their crowns,
> And push us from our stools.
> (3.4.78–82)

The twenty head wounds mentioned by the murderer provide fodder for Macbeth's musing out loud about bloody hair and exposed brains, but the hilarity of this remark, in his concern with a lost chair, creates an untenable jar for the guests and the audience.

The disorder of Macbeth's soul produced more macabre humor when he faced the ghost of his murdered friend:

> If charnal houses and our graves must send
> Those that we bury back, our monuments
> Shall be the maws of kites.
> (3.4.71–73)

Thus, when the ghost returns in response to Macbeth's hypocritical toast "to th'general joy o' th'whole table, / And to our dear friend Banquo" (3.4.89–90), Macbeth chides his murderee for no signs of life:

> Let the earth hide thee!
> Thy bones are marrowless, thy blood is cold;
> Thou hast no speculation in those eyes
> Which thou dost glare with!
> (3.4.93–96)

When Lady Macbeth says to her husband, "You have displaced the mirth, broke the good meeting / With most admired disorder" (3.4.109–110), she has precisely stated the case. The mirth of the banquet has been replaced by a macabre form of wit as Macbeth confronts Banquo's ghost in most "displaced" fashion. Thus the "admired disorder" of his conscience speaks out loud in his wholly or semi-interior monologues.

Montaigne pictures the inner soul of the public man who suffers from a bad conscience with the condemnation of his inner being:

> View him from within; there all is turbulent, disordered and vile. (252)

But in Macbeth's case the disorder takes the form of an odd Gothic sense of humor that parallels the cosmic laugh of such romantic protagonists as Melmoth the Wanderer, and, as I have suggested, some of the Porter's macabre humor. The Porter's hell has this odd element in common with Macbeth's conscience. Shakespeare has invented a peculiar kind of disorder in the diseased mind of Macbeth, not entirely explained in Montaigne. The internal leveling and disorder of elements of his mind are symbolized by hemoptysis and hemorrhage parallel to the bleeding of external trauma. That political damage seen in the Preface in Brutus's nightmarish internal condition has found its metaphor.

Macbeth muses on blood's demand for blood, blood, he suggests, that is inside of his head.

> I am in blood
> Stepped in so far that, should I wade no more,
> Returning were as tedious as go o'er.
> Strange things I have in head. . . .
>
> (3.4.136–39)

These musings, or overheard interior monologues, give a picture of Macbeth's conscience-stricken mind that follows the sense of the loss of all friendship with the loss of any brotherhood with man or oneness with the universe.

In "On Repenting," when he arrives at the notion that the world could be considered a stage where each human acts out predestined roles, Montaigne rebels and emphasizes that, if he enjoys a healthy conscience, man can maintain his reason and his free will and his peculiar personality in the face of all the plausibilities of determinist psychology. As I have shown, Montaigne emphasizes that self-examination need not be read in terms of seven-year stages, as found, for example, in Shakespeare's melancholic Jaques's acidic psychosociology. Montaigne even suggests that those roles may be insignificant, because they are conscious shows put on by free men merely for the outer world, a kind of successful jest and a piece of inexorable artistry. One should be aware of the innate freedom from roles adopted and should look to one's interior:

> Everyone may play the juggler and represent an honest man upon the stage; but within, and in bosom, where all things are lawful, where all is concealed, to keep a due rule or formal decorum, that's the point. (251)

Shakespeare, however, makes his picture of bad conscience in Macbeth reduce to *nihil* the concept of man's freedom.

When, near the end of the play, Macbeth is informed by Seyton—whose name suggests another tyrannous and inexorable evil force—of Lady Macbeth's apparent suicide, Macbeth launches his final semisoliloquy, which combines a concept of absolute determinism with a notion of the passage of time, now reduced to the flow of meaningless words. Macbeth is now dislocated both from good fellowship and from any significant link with operation of the cosmos:

> To-morrow, and to-morrow, and to-morrow
> Creeps in this petty pace from day to day
> To the last syllable of recorded time,
> And all our yesterdays have lighted fools
> The way to dusty death. Out, out, brief candle!
> Life's but a walking shadow, a poor player
> That struts and frets his hour upon the stage
> And then is heard no more. It is a tale
> Told by an idiot, full of sound and fury,
> Signifying nothing.
>
> (5.5.19–28)

In this overheard interior monologue, Macbeth denies the meaning of all those infinitesimally small increments of time Montaigne lauded for the development of the good conscience, and he rejects all creativity in roleplaying. He reduces the human struggle for identity to a predetermined process in which one ludicrously overacts, only to be waved, as Erasmus once said, off the stage by the manager, for bad acting.[8] If Montaigne emphasized a universe activated by the life of the soul, Macbeth sees its essence as a consciously "dusty" or "dusky" death in a play that operates in the twilight zone or uniform gray of bad conscience. Hardly a positive sign of Shakespeare's regard for his own dramatic art, the stage metaphor here, like the image of the bloody head inside and out, marks another stage in Macbeth's melancholic dislocation from the world, made eloquent by the saddest kind of wit.

The concept of the world as a stage turns out to be *melancholia's* heresy, because the healthy soul knows that the interior life is all. Both Shakespeare's Macbeth and Montaigne's *persona* in "Du Repentir" are deeply concerned with the concept of the passage of time. Ambitious, guilt-crazed Macbeth connects its movement strictly with destruction and death. All differentiation in the compartments of his soul yield to the wash of blood, and choice no longer exists. To the witches, he remarks in an odd conjuration suggesting time's awful damage:

> Though castles topple on their warders' heads,
> Though palaces and pyramids do slope
> Their heads to their foundations, though the treasure
> Of Nature's germains tumble all together
> Even till destruction sicken, answer me
> To what I ask you.
>
> (4.1.56–61)

Montaigne, near the opening of his essay, speaks only of his fascination with time's way of incrementally changing even the most durable things:

> The world turns all on wheels. All things therein move without intermission; yea the earth, the rocks of Caucasus, and the pyramids of Egypt, both with the public and their own motion. Constancy itself is nothing but a languishing and wavering dance. (248)

For Macbeth, with his bad conscience, an internal condition that levels the world he apprehends, that dance becomes a tortuous "strut and fret" leading only to his demise, a halting, universal dance of death. Bad conscience in Shakespeare, however, may not be the only cause of the soul's failure to distinguish and choose. As I hope to show in the case of the late romances, *The Winter's Tale* and *The Tempest*, the best ideals can have a similar effect in Shakespeare's picture of the human political animal.

PART 5
Ideal Solutions and Their Discontents

11

Shakespeare's Critique of the Mirage of the Green World in *As You Like It* and *The Winter's Tale*

Critics generally take Shakespeare's staging of idealism in love and politics as questionable, if not derogatory. Hugh Richmond, for example, once suggested that Shakespeare intentionally presents a Romeo, Claudio, or Othello as "naive,"[1] in love only to show how "admiratory" extravagance quickly transforms itself into violence and suicide. David Bevington and Jonathon Dollimore see Shakespeare's versions of utopian activism placed in such a pejorative context that they must, they claim, reflect prejudice in the playwright, his audience, and his age.[2] Clearly, English staged tragedy exposes the perils of egoism and egotism latent in political and erotic idealism from the day of Tamburlaine to that of the Giovanni of Ford's *'Tis Pity She's a Whore*. As in Sophocles' *Antigone*, English tragedy often pictures the heartrending fall of seekers of a better world. I argue, however, that Shakespeare no doubt creates icons of idealism and smashes them, but in order to show straining for perfection in both its best and worst clothes. Before I attempt to demonstrate Shakespeare's affective strategy, however, I would like to redefine the notion of the ideal in love and politics—in the latter case, I will use Empson's term "pastoral"[3]—in the universal political terms implied by Shakespeare's drama.

Man's most admirable goals go beyond self. Other than longing for personal gain, or success, or victory purely on an individual basis, one can hope for true love, which involves one other person, or for a pastoral world[4] in which many people are involved. This second transcendent ideal envisages a collective society, a new Eden or Isle of the Blessed, a green world where work is not work, where joint activity and sharing make human life for once supportable, without hierarchy and its concomitant police force. Some of human desire for this utopian paradise is focused on every daydream and soliloquy.

The goal, however, of such utopian enterprise is huge, and its attainment is complicated by human fallibility. Success is barely discernible. Human goals on the individual targeted level can often be quantified. Numbers can tell Macbeth if he is number one of a possible four, thereby for a moment making him immortal, or, rather, the "best" of humans and therefore the closest to gods, a king. When one comes to the ideal first true love and especially second true love and third true love, numbers are anathema, as Romeo comes to know, and his name comes to imply. Feelings only help. When it comes to transition to a collective pastoral world of *otium* and cooperation, only general consensus seems to be of any use in defining relative achievement. Sudden flashes of Adamic ease, perhaps, like those of even a self-flagellating King Lear in the wilderness.

Ideals create strain for the individual, as Shakespeare shows throughout his dramatic career. Idealistic tension can burst into sudden creation or destruction in a Hamlet or a Troilus. English tragedy may purge the audience of what Sidney called "admiration and commiseration"[5] through the spectacle of the vertiginous fall of a sequence of idealists who give high poetic voice to their unattainable dreams of perfection. When one observes a youth reaching for an ideal in life or on the stage, one admires, but worries. Man's or woman's ideals of true love and for the pastoral life naturally form the basis of their most creative activity, certainly the basis of most poetry. Samuel Johnson's famous attacks on some forms of love poetry like Cowley's and on pastoral poetry like Milton's *Lycidas*[6] may reflect a feeling that both ideals are false. Poets invented the lure of true love and pastoral harmony, and their audiences bit and were hooked. Thus three-quarters of all present-day rock songs—like Elizabethan lyrics—may be about unrequited love, but that does not mean that ideal "true love" exists. The other quarter, like "Electric Avenue," "Revolution," or "Don't Worry, Be Happy," "Under the Greenwood Tree," "Fear no more," or the Fool's songs of *King Lear*, may be about creating utopia, but utopia may remain an impossible human goal. In the first case, the one concerning mating, says my hypothetical Johnson, surely there is heat, but sexual attraction does not continue in one direction. Desire for novelty makes all humans unfaithful. Of course there is the creation of the family, but that operation is remote from true love, as the poets continually insist. What about the pastoral ideal? A figment of the imagination, Johnson might say, nourished by the pastoralists, based on poetic myths of paradise and perhaps on the puerile misunderstanding of how parents' money and rank protected children on their first summer vacation in the country, or at the seashore, or in the parks.

Let me, however, step beyond my cynical hypothetical Johnson for a moment. As shown in Shakespeare's drama, there is nothing more enticing to the human political animal, nor inevitable, than the ideal of true love or of pastoral harmony. The ideals will remain beautiful no matter how many banks and baby carriages are randomly blown apart, no matter how many first loves and Brook Farms die a natural death. Romeo remains equally beautiful, I argue, in his cries for true love with Rosaline and then Juliet, and in his willful ignorance of familial hostility, and in his ill-fated "utopian" attempt to join Mercutio and Tybalt in friendship. In fact, it may be that humans will not be capable of any good whatsoever unless they hold up the ideals of true love and the pastoral in front of them, even though those ideals may turn out to be perfectly "poetical" pieces of fancy, chimera that cause the mind's eye to blur. These perhaps illusory goals remain the great motivators as well as the stuff of poetry. Without such mystical ends in mind, the human being would wilt, decline, decay, and Shakespeare also makes this clear.

In this brief chapter, I would like to take a look at the desire for the pastoral world in all its beauty and also define the purported pitfalls and dangers of trying to bring into being something of the pastoral ideal as shown in Karl Marx, who espoused the ideal, and in Shakespeare, who criticized as he glorified it. I make this apparent digression into the realm of Hegelian philosophy in order to meet, once again, Shakespeare's materialist critics on their own ground. First, however, I would like to analyze a few aspects of the great Hebrew myth of Eden that, I argue, partly inspired both Marx's and Shakespeare's pastoral visions.

Desire for the pastoral ideal might lead one into a search for more Edenic weather, perhaps a golden world of eternal springtime. One might seek oneness with nature and pay less attention to the clock than to the length of light and dark in the day. Greenery helps. With some reservations, one seeks for a collective, classless, moneyless world on the beach or in the woods. One would choose to have no death, or at least the ability to forget about the imminence of death, no pain in childbirth, no work that felt like work, of course, no clothes sometimes. As a man, one might want as God-given companion a pre–serpent-influenced Eve with whom sexual politics were unnecessary. As a woman, one might want an unselfconscious Adam. What idealistic strain such a quest for the ideal creates! People typically say, on their return from a would-be idyllic vacation, "Now I can rest." Shakespeare's utopian adventurers always sigh with relief on their return home. And who knows how much strain and exhaustion are visited upon retirees, forced or otherwise, on the Duke Senior of *As You Like It,* or the Prospero of *The Tempest.* Mortality figures and poetic parables tell something. The weather fails. The idea of Eden strains one's natural-born political soul, engendering severe forms of melancholy. The Isle of the Blessed, the Terrestrial Paradise, may be too "good" for the human political animal.

On the other hand, desire for the utopian or pastoral ideal becomes, I believe, the human being's supreme motivator for the good. It is the focus of dreams, awake and sleeping. One remains for a moment in that ideal landscape when one awakens to surroundings, sometimes even to the point of becoming disoriented. It was and is a nice place—as the creators of Roman pastoral called it, a *locus amoenus,* where the amenities are located. Those amenities include leisure, recreation, a sense of immortality, and absolute genial rightness or absence of sin. In this chapter, let me briefly contrast active acquiescense of the pastoral ideal in the works of Marx with what I propose is criticism of it in William Shakespeare's *As You Like It* and *The Winter's Tale.*

Karl Marx, in "Romantic" edgy sarcasm, would like his audience to reconstitute a mythical "archaic" tribal situation of cooperation in the absence of exploitation, capital, and sometimes, currency exchange, where tribal members, living in a simpler world, owned but did not know they owned the means of production, which they shared with others in the archetypal commune. Sometimes he suggests this happy state was shared by the early Roman plebeian, before their land was expropriated by the state. He even suggests that contemporary primitive societies in India lived in nature with such a communal system, a system he chooses to call "Asiatic." But of course Marx's radical concern is to lead his audience into the future, beyond even the revolution that places the many in a position of absolute rule. That "dictatorship itself only constitutes the transition to the *abolition of all classes* and to a *classless society,*" he writes to his friend, Joseph Weydemeyer, in New York, in 1852.[7] What is beyond but the "withering away of the state," the reduced work day, perhaps pure recreation in the afternoon, the reunification with nature, the pastoral ideal? Would it be fair to say that Marx would have his follower espouse the ideal of Eden and then explode with all the energy, violent and creative, that the strain of not attaining that ideal will bring about? I think, in the terms I have stated, he would. Shakespeare is for less "romantic" and inclined to criticize not so much the people who are "used" by the ideal, but the availability of the ideal itself. Thus, in his high fictive mode, he can create parables of the human political animal that speak directly to the audience of what he represents as the clouding or blurring of perception that such idealism entails.

Shakespeare first takes a full-fledged look at the pastoral world at the age of thirty-four in his Forest of Arden in *As You Like It*. Those who associate this forest with bitter and bitterly cold battles of World War I or the "Battle of the Bulge" in World War II will be surprised to hear the supreme German categorizer of rhetorical commonplaces in early modern literature, Ernst Robert Curtius, say: "In Shakespeare's Forest of Arden (*As You Like It*) there are still palms, olives, and lions."[8] Arden is a version of the terrestrial paradise, the *locus amoenus*, the Edenic green world, now peopled by an exiled Duke Senior and his cohorts.

Shakespeare, however, by no means paints a rosy picture of the move to the would-be "utopian" green world of the retired Duke in his magical forest. In part, Duke Senior is in training in the forest to learn how not to be deposed, and the first thing he needs is a professor of human nature and a system of spies. One would think the collective society could do without the KGB, CIA, or queen's intelligence corps, but when the Duke first extols the forest far from the "envious court" (2.1.4), it is during a report from the Duke's subordinates on the doings and thoughts of the psychologist, Jaques. The Duke leads this collection of intelligence with "But what said Jaques?" (2.1.43). "And did you leave him in this contemplation?" (2.1.64), and then "Show me the place. / I love to cope him in these sullen fits, / For then he's full of matter" (2.1.66–68). And what is Jaques's matter but a wry criticism of the possibility of "going back to nature"? What he moralized is the death of a deer at the hand of one of the ex-Duke's hunters. According to Jaques, Duke Senior has merely moved the court into the woods, to kill the innocent denizens of the green world for food and sport. "Going back to nature," as it often does, might imply a return to the most predatory aspects of man. But that is hardly Edenic.

It is reported that

> Indeed, my lord,
> The melancholy Jaques grieves at that,
> And in that kind swears you do more usurp
> Than doth your brother that hath banished you.
> (2.1.25–28)

Bringing violent death to your brother stag is worse than banishing an older brother by comparison of execution to ostracism. You are not really creating a new paradise; you are exploiting the green world for personal profit or "expense." Jaques is of course filled with the poison of melancholy or black bile like his fellow Jacks in Shakespeare—Jack Falstaff, *Much Ado About Nothing*'s John, *Othello*'s Iago, and *Cymbeline*'s Iachimo—but though a former "libertine" (2.7.65), he makes a valid point. Duke Senior has largely moved his court into the country and has pronounced the dangerous mix pastoral leisure. Jacques may be suffering from incipient horror at eating meat—for Shakespeare, apparently, a manifestation of cosmic or religious melancholy—but stags would certainly have it better without hunters. Shakespeare is saying that humans, on the whole, are meat-eaters never at one with the more edible animals.

In the pastoral world the courtier Amiens sings

> Under the Greenwood tree . . .
> Here shall he see no enemy
> But winter and rough weather.
> (2.5.1, 6–7)

But the forest world has more enemies than stormy cold. Behold the lover Orlando cutting Rosalind's name into the innocent trees. Jacques is again on cue:

> I pray you mar no more trees with writing love songs in their barks. (3.2.247–48)

Even Rosaline points out that

> There is a man haunts the forest that abuses our young plants with carving "Rosalind" on their barks. (3.2.339–41)

Mirage of the Green World 123

Here the violence served nature comes not from efforts to establish the pastoral ideal but the ideal of true love, which is foreign to utopian possessionless cooperation. Ironically, Shakespeare turns this apparent paradise into Orlando's school of sexual politics. Near the end of the play, when Duke Senior is suddenly restored his lands, the audience is immediately returned from this would-be pastoral escape to city and court and hierarchy.

> And after, every of this happy number
> That have endured shrewd days and nights with us
> Shall share the good of our returnèd fortune,
> According to the measure of their states.
>
> (5.4.166–69)

Thus all was just "shrewd" or cold weather—Shakespeare will not let the audience forget that even his Arden has its winters—and all members of the former collective society must return to their hierarchical niche in society, "according to the measure of their states." What is the lesson? The ideal of paradise on earth is beautiful, maddeningly so, and the supreme motivation for cooperation, but hardly suitable to the human political animal. It causes humans to mistake their own nature, and it can lead to severe strife among its naive adherents. Having established this "point," Shakespeare takes a more comprehensive critical look at the pastoral ideal twelve years later, in 1610, in his penultimate play.

At one point, early in his late romance, *The Winter's Tale*, Shakespeare allows two of his characters to examine the pastoral ideal as a recurring memory of childhood in the green world. Hermione, the interrogator, wittily picturing boys as potential vandals and mischief-makers, asks her husband's oldest and best friend, Polixenes,

> Was not my Lord
> The verier wag o' th' two?
>
> (1.2.65–66)

Polixenes "answers" her not by denying that there was mischief, but that there was no consciousness on either part of wrongdoing. He applies to himself and his friend and "double" the elementary pastoral image of sheep.

> We were as twinned lambs that did frisk i' th' sun,
> And bleat one at th'other. What we changed

> Was innocence for innocence; we knew not
> The doctrine of ill-doing, nor dreamed
> That any did.
>
> (1.2.67–71)

One effect of living spiritually in an idealized green world, either as an early childhood image of sunny days away from school or as a psychic abode in some future world of leisure and sharing, is the absence of a personal sense of fallibility or sin that easily slips into "rigor" or despotism with one's fellows.

Polixenes wryly observes that

> Had we pursued that life,
> And our weak spirits ne'er been higher reared
> With stronger blood, we should have answered heaven
> Boldy "Not guilty," the imposition cleared
> Hereditary ours.
>
> (1.2.71–75)

Clearly if one returns, even in memory, to an Eden of childhood, one magically become presexual, immortal, and perfectly and innocently right in one's naming of things. One of the psychic effects of "living" in a pastoral land of the past or future is an urge to tyranny; who would not tyrannize who knew for sure he or she was right, who was self-consciously sinless?

Shakespeare proceeds to demonstrate absolute tyranny of opinion or "rigor" in Leontes' unfounded belief that his wife, Hermione, and his best friend, Polixenes, have been carrying on a nine-month affair under his eyes. This irrational tact leads to his decision to "expose" his wife's new born child. Note, however, that the beginning of the end, the seed of destruction, so to speak, of their green world, according to the protagonists, is woman. The "Eves" in Hermione's interrogation of Polixenes are Leontes' wife, Hermione, and Polixenes' unnamed spouse. Hermione sardonically queries Polixenes about his one-time felt denial of hereditary "original" sin.

> By this we gather
> You have tripped since.
> *Polixenes.* O my most sacred lady,
> Temptations have since then been born to's, for
> In those unfledged days was my wife a girl;
> Your precious self had then not crossed the eyes

> Of my young playfellow.
> *Hermione.*   Grace to boot!
> Of this make no conclusion, lest you say
> Your queen and I are devils.
>
> (1.2.75–82)

Indeed they are at least tempters if not devils in the context of the ideal of the green world. They had better remain girls. As women, their entry into the pastoral world introduces feelings of possession in the two boys. And possession leads to conflict in a now no longer collective paradise. The former twinned lambs become potentially the deadliest enemies; green worlds do not survive possession or possessiveness in the inhabitant. One's personal desire for sexual objects or gold lays a wintry pall on the springtime world of leisure and cooperation.

Shakespeare, later the *The Winter's Tale*, shows, in one of his most notorious vignettes, how gold can also bedevil the collective society of shepherds. Impossibly on the seacoast of Bohemia, Hermione's newborn child is exposed to the elements by the old counselor, Antigonus, who exits "pursued by a bear"; two shepherds looking for a lost sheep discover the child Perdita and, with her, one cries, "Gold! all gold!" (3.3.113). The shepherd responds, "This is fairy gold, boy, and 'twill prove so. Up with 't, keep it close. Home, home, the next way. We are lucky, boy, and to be so still requires nothing but secrecy. *Let my sheep go*" [italics mine] (3.3.114–17). Not only is the child neglected for the moment, but so are the sheep. Furthermore, the open-handed green world suddenly has secrets.

Is Shakespeare merely spoofing the idea of terrestrial paradise, picturing it as juvenile, unreconcilable to human nature? I think not. He knows this great social ideal, and he admires and imitates the poets like Virgil who developed it into a poetic commonplace. On the other hand, he subtly warns of the frustrations inherent in attempts to install such a paradise in the greater world of the human social and political animal, with personal interests most notably in the form of gold and sexual objects. Thus he admonishes his audience in moments of utopian idealism to remember bad weather, hierarchy, delusions of infallibility, the need for clothing, and all the other trappings of sexual politics. Without these internal warnings humans may lose their ability to distinguish elements of the actual world, and their own "will" may come to rule with all its irrational force.

Shakespeare's protagonists cannot forget the pastoral ideal any more than that of true love. Those ideals make up the fabric of all high poetry, yet they may, as I will show in the case of Prospero's Milan, cause one's identity, internal and external, to slip. Without a sense of difference, neither control nor freedom can exist.

12

Hierarchy and Freedom in the New World: Duke Prospero's Education in the Yare

Shakespeare generally painted a picture of monarchic states like the one he lived in, but not necessarily autocratic ones; the concept of necessary freedom and license or excessive freedom in a strictly hierarchical state or institution seems to have caught his fancy, a fancy that plays before his audience most forcibly, I think, in his last romance, *The Tempest*. "Tempest" suggests inexorable chaos in the Mediterranean or Atlantic Ocean, but this tempest can be negotiated, as the play makes clear. Prospero's and other storms in the play test one's maneuverability and direction. Chaos can be given order by tempering the rigors of autocracy with earned liberty, the absence of which, the Elizabethans and Jacobeans were proud to think, occurred only in tyrannical zones like Russia, Persia, and Spain.[1] What better image for overcoming chaos than the sailboat, a picture of order tempered by freedom, sailing on an angry sea?

The opening scene of Shakespeare's *Tempest*, though it is sometimes excised, or literally "drowned" by the noisy stage business of a storm at sea, like many Shakespearean beginnings, holds, I feel, the key to an understanding of the political schema of the play as a whole. The captain of a Neopolitan royal flagship orders a boatswain to work the mariners to keep the sailing ship off the shallows in rough water. The king of Naples, his courtiers, and a vassal duke of Milan arrive on deck to consult with the master, and are rudely told by the boatswain to go below or, indeed, work as mariners under his command. The courtiers grumble. The tempest rises. All seems lost.

This scene in part suggests that rank and power are relative. On land a king is a king, but on board a sailboat in a storm at sea, the captain is king, and his very boatswain enjoys superior rank not only to grumbling courtiers, but to the ruler of Naples himself. Essential to political order are recognition of one's rank in present circumstances and also realization of efficient rule suggested by a key word, "yare." This word is now a yachtsman's term for "smooth lines," "well-rigged," "quick to the helm," "yar,"[2] but to Shakespeare it also implies "quick," "efficient," a modifier suggesting also the very best rigging and lines and sailing of a ship of state, a state in which every element responds freely, and with alacrity to its function in all degrees, from jib to mainsail, from mariner to admiral, servant to hereditary monarch.

The boatswain receives orders from the captain: "Speak to th'mariners; fall to't yarely, or we run ourselves aground. Bestir, bestir! *Exit*" (1.1.3). "Yarely" here serves to suggest immediate and strict response to one's function in the ship. The boatswain now uses the term to rally the mariners: "Yare, yare! Take in the topsail! Tend to th' master's whistle!" (1.1.6)—until he is interrupted by King Alonso of Naples and his "un-yare" royal party, who the boatswain chides "I pray now, keep below" (1.1.10). In a failed attempt to keep the ship off the shoals, the boatswain shouts, "Down with the topmast! Yare!" (1.1.32), and the scene soon makes a radical shift.

Suddenly on a desert island the audience discovers a familiar "type" from Shakespeare's great tragedies, and a number of his comedies—the aging, wifeless, daughter-worshipping (and, of course, condemning), schoolmasterly Prospero, giving his 15-year-old daughter, Miranda, a bitter and oddly tortured lecture on his own education in the "yare," the efficient and good in government. Unlike other elderly widowers with marriageable daughters in Shakespeare—for example, the Polonius of *Hamlet* and the Brabantio of *Othello*—Prospero, I argue, is going to school at his advanced age, and unlike King Lear he will be able to use what he has so bitterly learned about sound principles of rule, the creation of a "yare" ship of state, here in his mandatory "retirement" on a desert island that suggests—with references to Bermuda and Indians—the new world of America and Virginia.

Back in Milan, as M. M. Reese long ago pointed out,[3] Prospero had remained quite "unyare." Fame of his great learning and desire to read deeply in occult science had led him to believe that he could exchange his identity as a duke for one of a scholar at leisure, a retiree, an entirely free man. After all, as the foremost individual in Milan, he was free simply to will a new identity for himself in the political hierarchy: he says of that "unyare" self, in a distant third person,

> And Prospero the prime duke, being so reputed
> In dignity, and for the liberal arts
> Without a parallel; those being all my study,
> The government I cast upon my brother
> And to my state grew stranger, being transported
> And rapt in secret studies.
>
> (1.2.72–77)

To Milan he became a foreigner, but also to his own "estate," his rank and identity. Prospero became the self-estranged monarch, the antinomy of tyrant, and far more dangerous. In his formal and schoolmasterly monologue—punctuated by such phrases as "Dost thou attend me?" (1.2.78) and "I pray thee, mark me" (1.2.88), which lead eventually to a drowsy Miranda dropping off by sheer somnolence, if not by magic—however, Prospero reveals that dukes must not become so free as to become full-time scholars and men of leisure. If they try, they actually become nothing, or rather, ex-Dukes in enforced early retirement in exile, often at crippling expense to the state and its heirs and citizens.

Brother Antonio, new Duke, arranges a coup d'état that includes selling Milan's sovereignty to Naples—"most ignoble stooping" (1.2.116)—and former Duke Prospero is put to sea with his daughter, Miranda, in a suitably unyare vessel,

> A rotten carcass of a butt, not rigged,
> Nor tackle, sail, nor mast; the very rats
> Instinctively have quit it.
>
> (1.2.146–48)

From confused and melancholic master of an "unyare" vessel, decking "the sea with drops full salt" (1.2.155), however, Prospero gradually becomes ruler of this desert island of the new world, master of arrangements of his daughter's marriage, and future duke of newly enfranchised Milan, quite logically abjuring the texts "I prize above my dukedom" (1.2.168) and other regalia of his occult science in the process of his "education" in rule.

Placed in this vessel, Prospero and Miranda arrive on an apparently deserted island, with the books of occult science, ironically, ready for an extended period—twelve years—of the life of leisure he had cut out for himself in Milan. But while he consciously trains himself as white magician and perfect "schoolmaster" (1.2.172) to his daughter, Prospero exerts the opposite of his slack mastery of Milan throughout the play; it is a most yare, efficient, Machiavellian (in the good sense) rule of the island that he exercises. He governs native (Caliban), daughter (Miranda), and spirit (Ariel) with flexible authority. The rigging is tight. His commands (even the famous one to the prince of Naples to carry wood) are immediately effected, or immediate punishment (such as paralysis of the same prince) is inflicted. The state is quick to the helm.

In such a hierarchy, the presence of freedom and the promise of freedom are essential ingredients. In fact, authority can enjoy no freedom until the subject is free to use initiative, and such response requires freedom to act. On the deck of the ship in the first scene, in King Alonso's happy phrase, one must "play the men" (1.1.9). Prospero enjoys a central relationship with his secretary of state, lieutenant, and servant spirit, Ariel, that shows that the rigging must have that same play.

As opposed to the implication of sometime female casting,[4] I feel Ariel must embody vigorous boyhood, mischief-loving—barking like a hound to terrify new arrivals on the island—girl-hating or, rather, sex-hating or, rather, intimacy-hating—he has been for twelve years confined by a witch Sycorax in a cloven pine because, in Prospero's sly words, he was a "spirit too delicate / To act her earthy and abhorred commands" (1.2.272–73).[5] Above all, Ariel, like the universal, would-be immortal boy, yearns to be free to roam at large in nature, in the green world of youth, and, of course, to rebel. Yet when he first appears in the play, he is most "yare":

> All hail, great master! Grave sir, hail! I come
> To answer thy best pleasure; be't to fly,
> To swim, to dive into the fire, to ride
> On the curled clouds. To thy strong bidding task
> Ariel and all his quality.
>
> (1.2.189–93)

Supremely disciplined, Ariel begs to be worked to his limits. He performs the roles of good servant, intelligence officer, and administrator with heart. He is the rigging of Prospero's ship of state. Yet he thrives on the promise of freedom. His second request to Prospero is "My liberty" (1.2.245), for which he is reminded of Sycorax's imprisonment. Yet rigging needs its play or it will lose its spring, or, perhaps, it will snap.

At one crucial moment of the play, I argue, Ariel demonstrates why a ruler must allow deserved freedom to his subjects. Without freedom and the promise of deserved promotion there will be no chance to perform to one's capacity, and there will be no creative leisure for the monarch, merely a prison of angry frustration. Caught up in the creation of a magical masque of gods and goddesses for Miranda and Ferdinand, Prospero suddenly realizes he has suffered an "unyare" moment of forgetfulness. He immediately becomes victim to a violent, angry mood that he tries to contain. The stage direction indicates that

> *Prospero starts suddenly and speaks; after which, to a strange, hollow, and confused noise, they* [the gods and goddesses] *heavily vanish.*
>
> Prospero. [aside] I had forgot that foul conspiracy
> Of the beast Caliban and his confederates
> Against my life.
>
> (4.1.139–41)

Ferdinand notices "your father's in some passion / That works him strongly." Miranda answers, "Never till this day / Saw I him touch'd with anger so distempered."

Prospero abstractedly misinterprets Ferdinand's reaction to his anger as amazement at the masque:

> You do look, my son, in a moved sort,
> As if you were dismayed: be cheerful, sir.
> Our revels now are ended.
>
> (4.1.146–48)

But he finally realizes the true cause and admits to him,

> Sir, I am vexed.
> Bear with my weakness: my old brain is troubled.
> Be not disturbed with my infirmity.
>
> (4.1.158–60)

What has disturbed Prospero so violently is his own "professorial" forgetfulness, that "unyare" or unready or inefficient noncontrol that once led to his failing to notice the former "foul conspiracy," that of his brother in Milan. Here again scholarly love of art and white magic has led him to ignore a plot on his life and his "state."

Confusion and anger overwhelm Prospero as they did when he so much as recounted the tale of Antonio's conspiracy to Miranda. Yet, thanks to his initiative, Ariel has taken the liberty to handle the problem alone. Thanks to his boyishly sadistic maneuvers, the conspirators are "dancing up to th' chins" (4.1.183) in mire. His protection of Prospero as well as its method were up to him. He was free to choose. When Ariel elaborates on his harrassment of the conspirators, Prospero's mood suddenly alters and he says to his lieutenant, "This was well done, my bird" (4.1.184). When the conspirators are literally hounded off the stage by Prospero and Ariel, Prospero reminds Ariel of his promise.

> Shortly shall all my labors end, and thou
> Shalt have the air at freedom.
>
> (4.1.263–64)

Without the promise of freedom to his lieutenant, Prospero will have no leisure to produce a masque. He will be permanently vexed by autocratic office. Yareness, like yar sailboats, always suggests simultaneous control and freedom.

When order is restored at the end of the play, and all are freed from their several autocratic bonds and prisons, the boatswain of the first act reappears to describe their sailing vessel:

> our ship,
> Which, but three glasses since, we gave out split,
> Is tight and yare and bravely rigged as when
> We first put out to sea.
>
> (5.1.222–25)

The ship of state is "yare" as well, and all Prospero's subjects, including the wayward Sebastian and Antonio and the still somewhat savage Caliban, are free to move unless they overstep the bounds of their present identity. To Caliban, Prospero's last words in the play are,

> As you look
> To have my pardon, trim it handsomely.
>
> (5.1.293–94)

One's freedom must always be as yare as a well-trimmed sail.

Shakespeare, who retired at the relatively young age of forty-six,[6] suggests that the world of freedom and leisure comes only when it is earned, and it remains a partial goal. In the state or the institution or the family, one must never lose a sense of one's identity and the need for control tempered with freedom symbolized by the "yare" ship. Therefore, in his Epilogue, Prospero demands the favorable breeze of applause to propel the sailboat of his genius back to Naples:

> Gentle breath of yours my sails
> Must fill, or else my project fails.
> (11–12)

If his boat sails well, then his final prayer to the audience may have validity.

> Let your indulgence set me free.
> (20)

Freedom, like grace, requires indulgence, and pardon, and love, too, as Ariel suggests, as well as deserving.

At an odd moment early in the play, the sanguine old counselor Gonzalo had thought that pure leisure and freedom were possible in the new world.[7] He would do away with all rank, distinction, and technology. He would forbid

> name of magistrate;
> Letters should not be known; riches, poverty,
> And use of service, none; contract, succession,
> Bourn, bound of land, tilth, vineyard, none;
> No use of metal, corn, or wine, or oil;
> No occupation; all men idle, all;
> And women too, but innocent and pure;
> No sovereignty.
> (2.1.145–52)

But this pastoral ideal, the supreme motivator to the good in politics, is not possible for man, and Gonzalo knows it. The state must be ruled. Thus Sebastian shrewdly points out,

> Yet he would be King on't.

And Antonio adds,

The latter end of his commonwealth forgets the beginning. (2.1.153)

Indeed, freedom comes only with control and self-control, Shakespeare "argues," if life is to be the maximal art of the "yare." Duke Prospero of Milan must become sovereign in order to be free.

Epilogue: Ulysses' Political Thoughts and Action in Reverse

Since 1945, when Una Ellis-Fermor, the editor of the invaluable Arden edition, last announced that Ulysses painted an ideal "ordered state" for the Greek council in *Troilus and Cressida*, a picture to parallel an "image of the ordered universe, of the cosmos with its regulated spheres,"[1] there has been little critical unanimity concerning this extended "political" speech and its potential for describing disorder as well as order, or, indeed, its implied dramatic motive in the soul of the Greek master of trickery. In order to explicate this oration, let me once again suggest how it provides clues to Shakespeare's own theory of the nature of the human political animal in social decline, and, also show how Ulysses can use elements of the process explained in his speech to turn back the clock of disorder in at least the Greek plot of the play.

One of the most compelling accounts of the logic of the oration—as opposed to its purported illogic[2]—lies in René Girard's brief analysis in *La Violence et le Sacré*. In a notable interpolation to Patrick Gregory's English translation of his text, Girard answers the argument that E. M. W. Tillyard,[3] Ellis-Fermor, and others propose with a question,

> To say this speech merely reflects a Renaissance commonplace, the great chain of being, is unsatisfactory. Who has seen a great chain of being collapse?[4]

Here, Girard argues that Ulysses does not speak of a rigid hierarchy but directly of a process that moves from loss of difference in rivalry to violent confrontation with one's fellows, to total dissolution and collective "sacrifice" of an arbitrarily chosen victim for the purpose of universal reconciliation. Throughout this book I have tried to show how Shakespeare posits elements of this process, a tragic decline that Ulysses, I argue, clearly expounds.

Ulysses describes a condition of leveling, or "undifferentiation," as Girard has it, in the Greek camp, where all difference, rank, identity, or degree is lost: "Th'unworthiest shows as fairly" (1.3.84) as the worthiest in the general masking. Rivalry, not a legitimate ruler, reigns over all: "Each thing meets / In mere oppugnancy" (1.3.110–11). Then "appetite, an universal wolf. . . . Must make perforce an universal prey / And last eat up himself" (1.3.121, 123–24). The words "universal" and "general" resound throughout. Although Ulysses is responding to Agamemnon, the Greek "general," about Achilles' "disobedience," he does not propose the imposition of a military "chain of command" that might echo some cosmic "chain of being." He is talking about a "general" process, notably in the gradual loss of identity that led up to "so many hollow factions" (1.3.80) in so many hollow "tents." The general's problem has become general, universal to the extent of creating disturbance in the stars.

When Girard closes his brief argument with a "translation" of Ulysses' own thought, "*reconciliez-vous ou punissez-vous les uns les autres,*"[5] however, I argue that he exaggerates the "tragic" in Shakespeare's resourceful Ulysses' political theory. As the odd epistle attached to the 1609 quarto proclaims, the play may well be a "comedy," or at least the Greek subplot is comic. For Girard the process of mimetic rivalry and collective violence points in only one direction, the one of total dissolution and total reconciliation. In fact, in Girard's theory, tragedy subsumes comedy, partly because all his scapegoats are elements of tragic process.[6] I argue that among the Greeks, Ulysses will reverse the process of decay. Stasis or reconciliation are not possible. From the dissolution he sees, Ulysses will bring protagonists like Ajax and Achilles, for example, backwards from dissolution and faction into what Girard calls reciprocal violence and mimetic rivalry, finally into a sense of their own identity and "degree." In other words, Ulysses will show that the process Girard so ably describes as moving solely in the direction of "sacrifice," can move in reverse, in a "comic" direction from dissolution and eventually reestablish identity, not through annihilation of the *pharmakos* but in the odd "marriage" of the victorious Greek constituents. Like Cassandra, I argue, Ulysses earnestly explains what his immediate audience does not hear. But if his explanation falls on deaf ears—except in the theater audience—he is free to activate the process by means of the indirection for which he is famous. Here, the constituents hear only too well.

Beyond the voice of the sonnets, if there is only one, Shakespeare's most developed analyst of the human political animal remains Ulysses, and yet, paradoxically, no voice in Shakespeare is more ventriloquist and Protean. In this council scene, I argue, Ulysses suspends his "Virgilian" indirection for a moment, and delivers an analysis of the breakdown of order that has no "trickery" in it. At this moment, however, Ulysses will, by a ruse that requires all his "voices," begin to reverse the process of political decay among his associates in the Greek camp. By means of benevolent deception, Ulysses gradually returns his camp to its political "senses," and, in the process, in one of his otherwise "darkest" moments, Shakespeare shows, for once, an Apollonian, not a Dionysian solution to the process of leveling.

In an odd inversion in his oration, Ulysses pictures the onset of a state of absolute leveling, saying that "Strength should be the lord of imbecility" (1.3.114). He really means the reverse, does he not, that imbecility should be the lord of all strength, that a strong idiocy would reign? However, his inversion actually suggests the reversal of the process that he plans to effect. If, as he says, "neglection of degree . . . goes backward with a purpose" (1.3.127), Ulysses will move the Greek camp "forwards" in the opposite direction, from "tented factions" to a notion of "degree." The solution lies in moving in reverse, as he suggests in his speech. Political decay can be corrected by inversion.

Ulysses ends his speech on the stage that precedes the final breakdown of social order. The previous moment in political decline was a plague, an "envious fever / Of pale and bloodless emulation" (1.3.133–34), engendered by a vacuum of power at the administrative level, Agamemnon's "place." Ulysses will move the Greeks back to that level. In his arranged "envious emulation" of Achilles and Ajax he will move the Greek camp one step backward toward political health. The ruse depends on deception. The parties must not know that Ulysses, with Nestor's help, is arranging the competition. This delicate process of reversion to a sense of hierarchy must be engineered by the master of false voices, the consummate artist of benevolent deception, Ulysses. His other great speech to Achilles, on the mutability of fame (3.3.145–89), for example, insincerely baits Achilles' envy and emulation. Only once in the play, I argue, is Ulysses heard to speak the simple political truth, but those words are, like the unwelcome prophet's, for the larger audience only. For the characters on the stage, Ulysses, the master of benevolent deception, must work through controlled images. Ulysses has spoken the truth, but it cannot be understood until he has set into motion his inverted process by indirection and manifested a kind of political health. Only then can Apollonian light shine, even in the mind of the uniquely comic scapegoat, Thersites, who seems to suspect Ulysses' design to enflame "the cur Ajax prouder than the cur Achilles" (5.4.14). Thus Shakespeare displaces all tragic elements in his Greek subplot and makes them comic, again showing how words and their distinctions may prove savior for his version of the human political animal.

Notes

Preface

1. All quotation from Shakespeare are cited by act, scene, and line number in the text and are based on *The Complete Pelican Shakespeare*, ed. Alfred Harbage (Baltimore: Penguin, 1969).
2. David Bevington, *Tudor Drama and Politics: A Critical Approach to Topical Meaning* (Cambridge: Harvard University Press, 1968), p. 249.
3. See chapter 9 for a discussion of the English and Sicilian parliamentary traditions. Elizabethan statesmen, such as parliamentarian Sir Edward Coke (1552–1634), not only emphasize the history of the Magna Carta and other guarantees of English liberties, but they also distinguish England's supposed "free" subject from that of more autocratic realms, such as the oft-maligned commonwealths of Russia or Persia. Sidney, in the second sonnet of *Astrophil and Stella*, compares his extreme plight in love to that of a "slave-borne Muscovite" (2.10) (*The Poems of Sir Philip Sidney*, ed. William A. Ringler, Jr. [Oxford: Clarendon, 1962], p. 166). In his *Epistle Dedicatorie* to *Of the Russe Common Wealth* (1591), the senior Giles Fletcher (ca. 1548–1611) juxtaposes the plight of Russian citizens living under tyranny with the happiness of her "majesties faithful subjects." When in *Paradise Lost* (1667), John Milton says Satan's throne "far / Outshone the wealth of Ormus" (2.1), among other implications, I believe he is metaphorically locating the throne of absolute tyranny in the Gulf of Hormuz, a far cry from England.
4. Warnings about the dangers of self-deposition of monarchs, contained in political parables in Sidney's *Arcadia* or in a number of Shakespeare's plays from *Henry VI* and *Love's Labor's Lost* to *Richard II*, *King Lear*, and the *Tempest*, appear throughout Elizabethan literature and political tracts. Such allegorical and expository animadversion aims, in part, I suspect, at the Spanish rulers' tendency to retire to religious retreat, in part, at a fear that Elizabeth may end up in doubtful deliberation with her own deputies in a time of crisis, such as during Philip II's long-planned invasion.
5. For a summary of discussion of paradoxical aspects of this passage, see Ronald Levao, *Renaissance Minds and Their Functions: Cusanus, Sidney, Shakespeare* (Berkeley: University of California Press, 1985), pp. 312–14.
6. For example, in direct reference to a rebellion in Elizabeth's days, the great Puritan theologian William Perkins (1558–1602) speaks of the Devil, Satan reproducing his own image in his "instruments" of mundane insurrection:

> We may see the truth here of in our owne land, in the manifold complots and treasons both at home and abroad, that have beene conspired and attempted against our Prince and State, by profane men stirred up by the Devill, through ambition and discontent: howsoever by Gods mercy themselves have beene taken in the snare that they laid for

others. . . . [God] hath brought to nought the devillish conspiracies & treacheries of the ambitious instruments of Satan.

The gloss notes, "Q. Elizabeth," *The Workes*, 3 vols. (London: John Haviland, 1631), 3:399.

7. See chapters 1 through 3.

8. See the discussion of Euripides' *Bacchae* in René Girard, *La Violence et le Sacré* (Paris: Bernard Grasset, 1972), pp. 180–208.

9. See, for example, Stephen Greenblatt, *Renaissance Self-Fashioning: From More to Shakespeare* (Chicago: University of Chicago Press, 1980); or Jonathan Dollimore's introductory essay to his and Alan Sinfield's edition, *Political Shakespeare: New Essays in Cultural Materialism* (Ithaca: Cornell University Press, 1985); and James Siemon, *Shakespearean Iconoclasm* (Berkeley: University of California Press, 1985).

10. Dollimore and Sinfield, ed., *Political Shakespeare*, p. 4.

11. Greenblatt, *Renaissance Self-Fashioning*, p. 256. Quoted by Dollimore in *Political Shakespeare*, p. 4.

12. Stephen Greenblatt, *Shakespearean Negotiations: The Circulation of Social Energy in Renaissance England*, The New Historicism: Studies in Cultural Poetics, no. 4 (Berkeley: University of California Press, 1988), p. 3.

13. See Annabel Patterson, *Censorship and Interpretation: The Conditions of Writing and Reading in Early Modern England* (Madison: University of Wisconsin Press, 1984), pp. 58–72; and Richard Strier and Heather Dubrow, eds., *The Historical Renaissance: New Essays in Tudor and Stuart Literature and Culture* (Chicago: University of Chicago Press, 1988), pp. 104–33, for Strier's essay, "Faithful Servants: Shakespeare's Praise of Disobedience." See also the essays in Gary Taylor and Michael Warren, eds., *The Division of Kingdoms: Shakespeare's Two Version of King Lear* (Oxford: Clarendon, 1983).

14. Sir Philip Sidney, *Miscellaneous Prose of Sir Philip Sidney*, ed. Katherine Duncan-Jones and Jan Van Dorsten (Oxford: Clarendon, 1973), p. 79, line 7.

15. Aristotle, *The Nicomachean Ethics*, trans. H. Rackhaun. Loeb Classical Library (London: Heinemann, 1934), p. 295.

Chapter 1. The Concept of the Machiavellian Ruler of Sonnet 94 and Its Discontents

1. William Empson opens his famous essay, "They That Have Power: Twist of Heroic-Pastoral Ideas into an Ironical Acceptance of Aristocracy." (*Some Versions of Pastoral* [London: Chatto and Windus, 1935], pp. 87–115), with the remark, "It is agreed that *They that have the power to hurt and will do none* is a piece of grave irony, but there the matter is generally left" (89). In spite of the impressionism of his paraphrases and statements—sometimes producing an uneven struggle with Thorpe's questionable punctuation—I remain influenced by his "black" Machiavellian interpretation, but I hold out for my "white" reading.

2. Quoted in Paul J. Alpers, ed., *Elizabethan Poetry: Modern Essays in Criticism* (Oxford: Oxford University Press, 1967), p. 287.

3. Stephen Booth, ed. and commentator, *Shakespeare's Sonnets* (New Haven: Yale University Press, 1977), p. 305.

4. Ibid., p. 309.

5. *The Complete Pelican Shakespeare*, p. 1468.
6. Booth, ed., *Shakespeare's Sonnets*, p. 308.
7. For example, A. P. Rossiter, in *Angel with Horns: And Other Shakespeare Lectures*, ed. Graham Storey (New York: Theatre Arts Books, 1961), p. 60, borrows the phrases "who, moving others are themselves as stone" and "lords and owners of their faces" and applies them to an analysis of a hereditary political indirection in Bolingbroke and Hal, but Rossiter, like Empson, is apparently describing what he sees as malevolent not benevolent political behavior. See chapter 3.
8. See, for example, Stephen Greenblatt's discussion of Shakespearean versions of improvisation in *Renaissance Self-Fashioning*, pp. 252–54, although Greenblatt makes no direct reference to sonnet 94.

Chapter 2. Teaching the Sly Animal to Be Civil

1. Peter Saccio briefly surveys the issue in "Shrewd and Kindly Farce," *Shakespeare Survey: An Annual Survey of Shakespearian Study and Production* 37 (1984): 33–40. Robert Ornstein suggests, to open his provocative interpretation, that the play is generally taken to be a "Punch-and-Judy farce in which a bully-boy hero imposes his will on a wild-eyed but ultimately supine heroine."(*Shakespeare's Comedies: From Roman Farce to Romantic Mystery* [Newark: University of Delaware Press, 1986], p. 63).
2. See the application of Henri Bergson's theory of the origins of laughter in Kevin L. Seligman, "Shakespeare's Use of Elizabethan Dress as a Comedic Device in *The Taming of the Shrew:* 'Something Mechanical Encrusted on the Living,'" *Quarterly Journal of Speech* 60 (1974): 39–44.
3. Joel Fineman, *Shakespeare's Perjured Eye: The Invention of Poetic Subjectivity in the Sonnets* (Berkeley: University of California Press, 1986), p. 126.
4. Shrews are not restrictively feminine. Witness, for example, Curtis's remark about Petruchio: "By this reck'ning he is more shrew than she" (4.1.77). In *Shakespeare's Perjured Eye*, Fineman sees a paradox of sexual exchange here, while I discover an "a-sexual" implication. *Taming of the Shrew*, I argue, applies equally to Sly and Kate and Grumio and Bianca. In the last case, I echo Harold C. Goddard, *The Meaning of Shakespeare* (Chicago: University of Chicago Press, 1951), p. 68, when he says, "Bianca, on the other hand, is just what her sister is supposed to be."
5. Interpretations of "pheese" reflect, I believe, a tendency of some editors of Shakespeare to make general or abstract sometimes crude or shocking meaning. While OED "a.", quoting Shakespeare's Sly yields "*vaguely*, To 'do for,' 'settle the business of' (a person), OED "b." goes on to provide "To beat, flog," a verbal form of the noun "feeze" whose first meaning from Chaucer's time was always "violent impact." Furthermore, if the word also picks up a connotation of similar sounding words of the period, I would suggest "face" or "physiognomy," rather than the tepid (and relatively recent) "faze" suggested, for example, by Robert B. Heilman in Silvan Barnet, gen. ed., *The Complete Signet Classic Shakespeare* (New York: Harcourt Brace Jovanovich, 1972). Of course, a shrew of a man offering a woman—even a rough and tumble hostess angered by the broken glasses on her hands—physical violence, especially to her face, understandably shocks the audience into wanting it unsaid, especially in the opening words of what promises to be a romantic comedy.

6. For example, Maynard Mack's wonderful discussion of "thrusting identities" on characters in the play refers largely to Sly and Kate as victims ("Engagement and Detachment in Shakespeare's Play," in *Essays on Shakespeare and Elizabethan Drama in Honor of Hardin Craig*, ed. Richard Hosley [Columbia: University of Missouri Press, 1962]). E. M. W. Tillyard, in *Shakespeare's Early Comedies* (New York: Barnes & Noble, 1965), p. 89, touches on this problem by saying that early critics "assumed that the main plot is more free and natural and that the subplot [the Bianca/Lucentio plot], because cast in a highly conventional mould, must therefore be inferior." Relegating the Bianca plot to subplot may perpetuate the prejudice that certainly has affected performance. Generally speaking, the Minola family forms the main plot of Sly's cautionary play.

7. See Maynard Mack's essay in *Essays . . . in Honor of Hardin Craig*, pp. 279–80.

8. For this interpretation, I am indebted to Rolf Soellner, who responded to an early version of this chapter delivered at the Sixteenth Century Studies Conference at Columbus, Ohio, October 1985.

Chapter 3. From Hal to Henry V

1. Rossiter, *Angel with Horns*, p. 60.

2. The *Henriad*, as it is called, the second tetralogy spanning *Richard II*, *1 Henry IV*, *2 Henry IV*, and *Henry V*, has often been called the true British epic, normally in comparison with *Paradise Lost*, which is not national, and *The Faerie Queene*, which is not, it has been claimed, epic, exactly, but epic-romance. In his great defence of *Henry V*, for example, M. M. Reese says, "Epic praises heroes and denouces villainy . . . epic is the art that on special occasions transforms it [human virtue] into the ideal" (*The Cease of Majesty: A Study of Shakespeare's History Plays* [London: Edward Arnold, 1961], pp. 321–22). I argue that Hal becomes a convincing epic hero, another Aeneas, for example, not for his perfection but for his "elegiac" sense of conquest that makes his audience uncertain it was all worth it.

3. William Butler Yeats, for example, found it so. See his *Essays and Introductions* (New York: Macmillan, 1961), p. 108.

4. Reese, *The Cease of Majesty*, p. 331.

Chapter 4. "Remorse in Myself with His Words"

1. For an entertaining argument for the coherence of *The Book of Sir Thomas More*, as well as a discussion of the scholarly background, as well as "foreground" (among Professors Howard-Hill, Melchiori, and others), see Scott McMillin, *The Elizabethan Theatre and "The Book of Sir Thomas More"* (Ithaca: Cornell University Press, 1987), especially chap. 7, pp. 135–59.

2. R. W. Chambers, "The Expression of Ideas—Particularly Political Ideas—in the Three Pages, and in Shakespeare," in *Shakespeare's Hand in the Play of Sir Thomas More*, ed. Alfred W. Pollard (Cambridge: Cambridge University Press, 1923), p. 156.

3. Bevington, *Tudor Drama and Politics*, p. 239.

4. Richard D. Fly, " 'Suited in Like Conditions as Our Argument': Imitative Form in Shakespeare's *Troilus and Cressida*," *Studies in English Literature*, 15 (1975): 291.

5. Jonathon Dollimore, *Radical Tragedy: Religion, Ideology and Power in the Drama of Shakespeare and His Contemporaries* (Chicago: University of Chicago Press, 1984), p. 44.

6. William H. Matchett, "Shylock, Iago, and *Sir Thomas More*: With Some Further Discussion of Shakespeare's Imagination," *PMLA* 92 (1977): 218.

7. See n. 1. Also see R. W. Chambers, "Shakespeare and the Play of *More*," in *Man's Unconquerable Mind* (London: Jonathan Cape, 1939), pp. 204–49; Karl P. Wentersdorf, "Linkages of Thought and Imagery in Shakespeare and *More*," *Modern Language Quarterly* 34 (1973): 384–405. All are referred to by Matchett as well.

8. The passage from More appears in *Shakespeare's Hand in the Play of Sir Thomas More*, p. 211. Cited hereafter by page number in the text.

9. Bevington, *Tudor Drama and Politics*, p. 240.

10. Ibid., p. 239.

11. René Girard has influenced my reading in his analysis of Ulysses' speech in *La Violence et le Sacré*, pp. 77–80.

12. Bevington, *Tudor Drama and Politics*, p 240.

13. "In the end, to be short (for the tale is notorious, and as notorious that was a tale), with punishing the belly they plagued themselves. This applied by him wrought such effect in the people, as I never read that only words brought forth but then so sudden and so good an alteration" (Sidney, *Miscellaneous Prose*, p. 93).

14. In this regard, see Annabel Patterson's discussion of *Richard II* and the two versions of *King Lear* in her *Censorship and Interpretation*.

Chapter 5. "The Teeth of Emulation"

1. Originally published in *PMLA* 66 (1951): 765–74, the paper was revised by Sterling into a chapter of his *Unity in Shakespearian Tragedy* (New York: Columbia University Press, 1956), pp. 40–54, and it appears *in toto* in Leonard F. Dean, ed., *Twentieth Century Interpretations of Julius Caesar* (Englewood Cliffs, N.J.: Prentice-Hall, 1968), pp. 39–56. I quote from the last work, on p. 40.

2. Philosophical, anthropological, and psychoanalytic interpretations of the play, for example, tend to emphasize the sacrificial theme but with little unanimity on its significance. Kenneth Burke early noted that the play concerns sacrificial crisis in "Antony in Behalf of the Play," in *The Philosophy of Literary Form* (Baton Rouge: Louisiana University Press, 1941), pp. 329–43. Norman Holland sees occult references to Christian archetypes in "The 'Cinna' and 'Cynicke' Episodes in *Julius Caesar*," *Shakespeare Quarterly* 11 (1960): 439–44. Peter S. Anderson, in "Shakespeare's *Caesar*, The Language of Sacrifice," *Comparative Drama* 3 (1969): 3–26, examines sacrificial displacement in terms, on the whole, of Claude Lévi-Strauss's structural anthropology. Henry Ebel, in "Caesar's Wounds: A Study of William Shakespeare," *Psychoanalytic Review* 62 (1975): 107–30, analyzes the work in terms of Sigmund Freud's anthropological theories expounded in *Moses and Monotheism* (*Totem and Taboo* also gives this material). While the latter essays provide lucid ethological studies of Shakespeare's versions of sacrifice in *Julius Caesar*, the connection

between rivalry and group violence remains obscure, in part, because Anderson and Ebel take Shakespeare's Caesar to be Brutus's father; this is Plutarch and Suetonius, not Shakespeare. Ralph Berry points out in "*Julius Caesar:* A Roman Tragedy," *Dalhousie Review* 61 (1981): 325, that "Shakespeare makes no use of the tradition that Brutus was Caesar's son—if anything, he preserves the suggestion of a son role for Anthony (III,i,22)." Lynn de Gerenday's intelligent article "Play, Ritualization, and Ambivalence in *Julius Caesar*," *Literature and Psychology* 24 (1974): 24–34, generally argues for "Freudian" ambivalence in the play's major figures and their speeches. More recently, Naomi Conn Liebler, in " 'Thou Bleeding Piece of Earth': The Ritual Ground of *Julius Caesar*," *Shakespeare Studies* 14 (1981): 175–96, argues that Shakespeare's incorporation of "Saturnalian" ritual imagery in the play, originally found in Plutarch's "Life of Romulus," is meant to reinforce for Shakespeare's audience the theme of decay of Roman custom through the crass politicization of traditional rites, rites similar to those found, for example, in Warwickshire in the sixteenth century. David Kaula, in " 'Let Us Be Sacrificers': Religious Motifs in *Julius Caesar*," *Shakespeare Studies* 14 (1981): 197–214, argues that ritual imagery in the play creates for Shakespeare's audience a version of the troubled contemporary world of Christianity, notably the polarization of Puritan and Papist. Both Liebler and Kaula elucidate legitimate historical and ethnic themes in the play, Roman and English. I choose to restrict my inquiry to the play's definition of the sacrificial process, its ethos. Liebler's discovery of the influence of Plutarch's first Roman life reminds one that the eternal city in Roman myth (like the first city in *Genesis*) was founded by a fratricide who was also a marked man. Plutarch's "Romulus" revolves around the general problem of violent rivalry and civil disturbance as well as ethnic themes.

3. In the chapter, "The Eroticism of *Julius Caesar*," in G. Wilson Knight, *The Imperial Theme* (London: Methuen, 1931), pp. 62–95.

4. The Lupercal is a Saturnalian holy day. On the Lupercal, as Liebler points out, "Rome's most ancient festival of purgation and fertility" ("Thou Bleeding Piece of Earth," p. 175), "Lupercians which rome about the cittie, doe also sacrifice a dogge" (Thomas North, trans., *Plutarch's Lives*, ed. W. E. Henley and George Windham, 6 vols. [London: David Nut, 1895], 1: 99). While North's Plutarch goes on to suggest that the dog is an enemy to the wolf, or, indeed, to the naked runners, I would guess that the dog is a version of the wolf and, by extension, of Mars, the Roman wolf-god. Liebler, in " 'Thou Bleeding Piece of Earth,' " p. 183, says about a goat sacrifice and the dabbing of two boys' heads with the blood: "But the cutting up of the sacrificial *pharmakos*, whose blood is smeared upon the flesh of the priestly celebrants, is one of the central events in the rites of the Lupercalia." Although Caesar no doubt includes these rites when he says "leave no ceremony out" (1.2.11), Lupercalian sacrifice is unmentioned in the play, though the smearing of blood forcibly reminds of the aftermath of the "sacrifice" of Caesar.

5. See Hugh Richmond, *Shakespeare's Political Plays* (New York: Random, 1967), Bevington, *Tudor Drama and Politics*, and Norman Rabkin, *Shakespeare and the Common Understanding* (New York: Free Press, 1967).

6. Richmond, *Shakespeare's Political Plays*, p. 207.

7. See Hugh Richmond, "Shakespeare's Roman Trilogy: The Climax in *Cymbeline*," *Studies in the Literary Imagination* 5 (1972): 129–40.

8. A fund of images, metaphors, and quibbles in the play suggest dissolving identity in both the patrician and plebeian party. By means of homonymic and

metathetic connection, the "mettle" or "metal" of human identity (including Metellus's) is pictured as "melting" when panic or other collective human response occurs. For example, as soon as the commoners leave, Flavius remarks, "See, whe'r their basest mettle be not moved" (1.1.61). Loss of identity is brought about by "that which melteth fools—I mean, sweet words" (3.1.42). Metellus, a minor character, appears by name in the text an extraordinary number of times (13) as if for word echo, even when he is speaking his few lines: "Metellus Cimber throws before thy seat / An humble heart" (3.1.34–34). Perhaps the cobbler may be seen as introducing such word play when he defiantly claims, "I meddle with no tradesman's matters" (1.1.21).

9. The speech also echoes one of Juliet's most powerful soliloquies (*Romeo and Juliet*, 2.2.38).

10. Imitation of Caesar by Brutus is discussed in Bevington, *Tudor Drama and Politics*, p. 249: "Although Brutus searches his motives for the deed [the murder], he never begins to suspect the extent to which he resembles Caesar." Also Norman Rabkin, "Common Characteristics of Brutus and Caesar," *Journal of English and Germanic Philology* 63 (1964): 241: "the Audience should be troubled by a sense of déjà vu," in reference to act 1, scene 2.

11. Curt A. Zimansky, ed., *The Critical Works of Thomas Rymer* (New Haven: Yale University Press, 1956), p. 168.

Chapter 6. Publishing the Politics of Literary Expropriation

1. In 1946, E. M. W. Tillyard says of the second tetralogy in contrast to the first: "In the first tetralogy the Tudor myth and the Morality idea of Republica had been the great unifying motives. In the second the epic idea is added to them" (*Shakespeare's History Plays* [New York: Macmillan, 1946], p. 242). This idea has experienced steadfast currency ever since. See especially David Riggs, *Shakespeare's Heroical Histories: "Henry VI" and Its Literary Tradition* (Cambridge: Harvard University Press, 1971).

2. Tillyard points out in *Shakespeare's History Plays* that "there is a variety of style, fully mastered, which is new in Shakespeare and which can hardly be matched even in his later work" (p. 295).

3. Tillyard says, "Falstaff commands not only the most exquisite conversational vein but the Euphuism of Lyly" (*Shakespeare's History Plays*, p. 248).

4. Robert Greene, *Groats-VVorth of Witte, bought with a million of Repentance*, 1592. The Bodley Head quartos, ed. G. B. Harrison (London: E. P. Dutton, 1923), pp. 45–46. Shakespeare's supposed feud with Greene may have had a happy ending in Shakespeare's close adaptation of *Pandosto* in *The Winter's Tale*, eighteen years after Greene's tragic death in 1592.

5. *The Complete Works of Christopher Marlowe*, ed. Fredson Bowers, 2 vols. (Cambridge: Cambridge University Press, 1973), cited hereafter by volume and page number in the text.

6. For a discussion of this connection, see Horace Howard Furness, ed., *Hamlet*, New Variorum Edition, 2 vols. (Philadelphia: J. Lippincott, 1905), 1: 181–89.

7. Ibid. Also see Bowers, ed., *The Complete Works of Christopher Marlowe*, ed. 60–61.

8. Sidney, *Miscellaneous Prose*, cited hereafter by page and line number in the text.

9. *The Complete Poetry of Ben Jonson*, ed. William B. Hunter, Jr., Anchor Books (Garden City, N.Y.: Doubleday, 1963), p. 373. At the close of line 30 of "To the Memory of My Beloved, the author William Shakespeare," prefixed to the First Folio.

10. Tillyard champions Lyly's dialogue. See n. 3. The best argument for the coherence of Lyly's prose style remains Jonas Barish's Spitzerian account, "The Prose Style of John Lyly," *ELH* 23 (1956): 14–35.

11. *The Complete Works of John Lyly*, ed. R. Warwick Bond, 3 vols. (Oxford: Clarendon, 1902), 1: 195–96.

Chapter 7. Exorcising the Moral Jonsonian Citizen Comedy in Shakespeare's *Twelfth Night, or, What You Will*

1. Paul Mueschke and Jeanette Fleisher, "Jonsonian Elements in the Comic Underplot of *Twelfth Night*," *PMLA* 48 (1933): 722–40.

2. In his folio, Jonson lists Shakespeare first among the actors in the opening performance of *Every Man in His Humour*.

3. First folio, *The Workes of Beniamin Jonson* (London: William Stansby, 1616). 2 vols. 1:3. Cited by line number in the text.

4. Notably Feste's probable jab at Jonson favoring the word "element": "my welkin; I might say 'element,' but the word is over-worn" (3.1.56), but Mueschke and Fleischer find elaborate references in "Jonsonian Elements in the Comic Underplot of *Twelfth Night*."

5. The problem of the separate action of the so-called "underplot" of *Twelfth Night* has received sporadic attention from the time of Mueschke and Fleishcer's article, which was primarily aimed at locating Shakespeare's sources, through Harry Levin's article "The Underplot of *Twelfth Night*," in *De Shakespeare à T. S. Eliot: Melanges offerts à Henri Fluchère*, ed. Marie-Jean Durry, Robert Ellrodt, and Marie Therèse Jones-Davies, Etudes anglaises 63 (Paris: Didier, 1976), pp. 53–59, which more or less underscores the validity of C. L. Barber's "Saturnalian" ritual interpretation of the plot of *Twelfth Night*, set forth in *Shakespeare's Festive Comedy: A Study of Dramatic Form and Its Relation to Social Custom* (Princeton: Princeton University Press, 1959). Marvin Herrick provides an interesting summary of Renaissance ideas on the plot of comedy in *Comic Theory in the Sixteenth Century* (Urbana: University of Illinois Press, 1950).

6. Jonson's form comes, in part, from Italy, where writers from Machiavelli to della Porta developed the gull-catching action, normally as subplot. Jonson promoted the Italianate con game to main plot and made it most contemporary, a symbol of his "city."

7. Ben Jonson, *Complete Poetry*, ed. William B. Hunter Jr., Anchor (Garden City: Doubleday, 1963), p. 387, Second "Ode to Himself," ll. 21–22.

8. Wayne Booth, *The Rhetoric of Fiction* (Chicago: University of Chicago Press, 1961), p. 260.

9. Edward Albee eyes this symbolic location—as a place to discover sexual identity?—when he has George announce, "this is your heart's content—Illyria" in *Who's Afraid of Virginia Woolf?*

10. Normally emended, by authority of alternate spelling, into "human." I

prefer "humane," meaning "as befits a man." Man's vain follies are thus opposed to "beastly" (or "criminal") ones. Men are capable of beastly (or criminal) follies, but they are not a proper subject of comedy. In OED 1, "humane" is traceable to 1500.

11. Quoted from the first folio, p. 3.

12. Such naming is, of course, a characteristic of the genre. Volpone's "big fox" and Mosca ("fly") suggest sly and predatory, or parasitical. The gulls' names, Corbaccio ("crow"), Corvino ("raven"), Voltore ("vulture"), suggest, like "gull" itself, simply predatory birds. Lady and Sir Politic Would-be are self-explanatory. By name, celestial Celia is probably not a suitable gull.

13. The "gull" in the English-speaking world has experienced a symbolic transformation of meaning, by way of the Russian input of Chekhov's (and Stanislavski's) Nina Mikhailovna into the noble wide-eyed, individualistic Jonathon Livingston Seagull and his fellows. But for the Elizabethans, he was gullible. Was it his gaping beak, his seeming idiotic reiterate caw? Or was it his tendency—though given some of Lady Nature's best eyesight and dexterity—to go for a silly man-made lure, one that was not even designed for him, but for the larger fish. In this sense a gull is simply stupid in his own hunting. He must hunt to eat and live, and yet he is a likely victim of life given his nature. Luring and catching this gull would not be "moral" if his disability were not self-willed. The victimized gull of the citizen comedy is made gullible by folly and affectation. Thus, he is more like the common man.

14. Booth, *The Rhetoric of Fiction*, p. 246.

15. See, for example, Botticelli's *Venus and Mars*.

16. It seems worth asking whether the Lord Chamberlain's men had twin boys to play the two parts.

17. For example, in Toby's remark on Andrew's failure to assail Maria: "An thou let part so, Sir Andrew, would thou mightst never draw sword again" (1.3.56).

18. First folio, p. 446.

19. Recall that Samuel Taylor Coleridge saw the plot of *The Alchemist*, with that of *Oedipus Rex* and *Tom Jones*, as the three "perfect" ones.

20. Aristotle *Poetics* 51b19–51b33, 53a12–53a30, and 53b26–54a16.

Chapter 8. Sacrificing the Mysteries

1. I here take Cassius's words out of context—out of time frame and other forms of relevance—and create an unauthorized mosaic. Yet, as I have argued above, Cassius holds all the pieces of a puzzle, but his "thick" (5.3.21) vision does not allow him to fit them together.

2. Even John Dryden will find himself compelled to justify using "spirits" in the face of Thomas Rymer's "ferocious . . . insistence on factual probability" and imitation of nature, the new standard (Robert D. Hume, *The Development of English Drama in the Late Seventeenth Century* [Oxford: Clarendon, 1976], p. 169).

3. John Dennis, *Critical Works*, 2 vols. (Baltimore: Johns Hopkins University Press, 1939–43), 2: 286, quoted also in Hume, *Development of English Drama*, pp. 152–53.

4. Eric Rothstein, *Restoration Tragedy: Form and the Process of Change* (Madison: University of Wisconsin Press, 1967), p. 3.

5. In *Ben Jonson*, ed. C. H. Herford and Percy and Evelyn Simpson (Oxford: Clarendon, 1947), 11 vols., 8: 390–92.

6. Facsimile in S. Schoenbaum, *William Shakespeare: A Compact Documentary Life* (New York: Oxford University Press, 1977), p. 267.

7. Samuel Johnson, in *Johnson on Shakespeare*, ed. Walter Raleigh (Oxford: Oxford University Press, 1908), p. 179.

8. See John W. Velz, comp., *The Tragedy of Julius Caesar: A Bibliography to Supplement the New Variorum Edition of 1913* (New York: MLA, 1977), and his *Shakespeare and the Classical Tradition: A Critical Guide to Commentary, 1660–1960* (Minneapolis: University of Minnesota Press, 1968).

9. Schoenbaum, *William Shakespeare*, p. 257.

10. From *Timber or Discoveries*, in Herford and Simpson, eds., *Ben Jonson*, 8: 584. T. S. Dorsch points this out in his introduction to the Arden Edition of *Julius Caesar* (London: Methuen, 1955), pp. ix–x. Jonson also parodies the remark in the induction to *The Staple of News*, 11. 36–37. Lady Prologue says to Lady Expectation, "Cry you mercy, you neuer did wrong, but with iust cause." Herford and Simpson, eds., *Ben Jonson*, 6: 280. See John Dover Wilson's summary of the problem in "Ben Jonson and 'Julius Caesar'" *Shakespeare Survey* 2 (1949): 36–43.

11. The notion of "satisfaction," especially of the appetite for blood when "honor" is at stake, is, however, consistent with the theme of vendetta in the play.

12. See Wilson, "Ben Jonson and 'Julius Caesar,'" p. 36, on this point.

13. Herford and Simpson, eds., *Ben Jonson*, 8: 583–84.

14. Zimanky, ed., *The Critical Works of Thomas Rymer*, pp. 165–67.

15. Oliver Lawson Dick, ed., *Aubrey's Brief Lives* (London: Secker & Warburg, 1960), p. 275.

16. G. Blakemore Evans, "The Problem of Brutus: An Eighteenth-Century Solution," in *Studies in Honor of T. W. Baldwin*, ed. Don Cameron Allen (Urbana: University of Illinois Press, 1958), p. 233.

17. Ibid., p. 231.

18. Ibid., p. 236. John Sheffield, *The Tragedy of Julius Caesar, Altered* (1722), in *The Works of John Sheffield, Duke of Buckingham* (London: John Barber, 1723), 2 vols., 1: 226–27.

19. Sheffield's second part anounced as *The Tragedy of Marcus Brutus* on the frontispiece, but thereafter referred to in the page titles as *The Death of Marcus Brutus*, is, on the whole, a political and moral justification of Brutus in the assassination of Caesar and in his relationship with Portia, which overshadows somewhat the other action. His apparent lack of a tragic flaw, or *hamartia*, not only brings into question, for the neoclassic, the appropriateness of his end but also raises the question of whether that end is tragic or merely a "death."

20. Sheffield, *The Tragedy of Julius Caesar, Altered*, 1: 294, "The Deed is done, what need we triumph in it?"

21. He will edit "with a religious abhorrence of all Innovation, and without any indulgence to my private sense of conjecture" (Alexander Pope, ed., *The Works of Shakespeare in Six Volumes* [London: Jacob Tonson, 1725], 1: xxii).

22. Pope's justification, though he admits that "in all the editions this speech is ascrib'd to *Brutus*," is that "nothing is more inconsistent with his [Brutus's] mild and philosophical character. But (as I often find speeches in the later editions put into wrong mouths, different from the first-publish'd by the author) I think this liberty not unreasonable" (ibid., 5: 285n). Malcomb Goldstein, in "Pope, Sheffield, and Shakespeare's *Julius Caesar*," *Modern Language Notes*

71 (1956): 8–10, argues the possible influence of Sheffield on Pope, but he does not trace back to Rymer's objection to Brutus's "bathing" exhortation.

23. As I mentioned in Chapter 5, n. 2, however, such analyses "miss" the connection between competition and crowd-forming, in part because they tend to take Shakespeare's Caesar to be Brutus's father; this is as I have shown, Plutarch and Suetonius, not Shakespeare, as one neoclassical critic pointed out. In the anonymous "Remarks upon the Tragedy of *Julius Caesar*," *British Magazine* 8 (1767): 571–74, where certain then conventional "blemishes" are found in the play, one finds:

> The celebrated Mons. de Voltaire, in his tragedy of Julius Caesar, has copied the whole speech of Antony, and followed Shakespear in many particulars; he has, however, differed from him in making Brutus the real son of Julius Caesar, which I cannot but think ill-judged, as it brings the odium of parricide upon the patriot. (p. 573)

Chapter 9. England's Sicily and Shakespeare's Critique of Gallantry in *Much Ado about Nothing*

1. Tina Whitaker, *Sicily through the Ages* (New York: Dutton, 1926), p. 3.
2. Thomas Brown visited the court of Ruggiero I, at Henry II's bidding, returned, and apparently introduced English authorities to the Sicilian treasury system, which was then adopted.
3. Whitaker, *Sicily through the Ages*, p. 10.
4. Helmut Koenigsburger, *The Practice of Empire* (Ithaca: Cornell University Press, 1969), p. 196.
5. John Aubrey claims that Shakespeare had trouble with a constable named Dogberry at Grendon and proceeded to "stage" him in revenge.
6. One of the central events behind this popular myth remains the massacre of 2,000-odd French men, women, and children in the so-called "Sicilian Vespers," on Easter Monday, 30 March 1282, traditionally laid at the door of disrespect shown a Sicilian woman by French soldiers outside the church of San Spirito in Palermo.
7. Koenigsburger, The Practice of Empire, p. 191.
8. Ibid., p. 188.
9. One of the many contemporary references to the events surrounding Marc Antonio Colonna's death occurs in French diplomatic papers from Madrid in the period, found in *Depêches Diplomatiqes de M. de Longlée, Résident de France en Espagne (1582–1590)*, ed. Albert Mousset (Paris: Plon-Nourrit, 1912). Longlée wonders why the loyal Roman, Colonna, a commander at Lepanto, was recalled. He puzzles over whether Philip II wanted a Spaniard in Sicily, remarks on the passage of money for a buildup of Spanish power in Italy and on Colonna's tension with Andrea Doria, and says that news of Colonna's death, from a fever on the road from Barcelona to Madrid, was received by the king on the same day as news of the assassination of William of Orange at Delft. Thus Philip II's grief was balanced by joy and vice versa. Longlée's final analysis indicates that the admiral (probably in line to command the Armada) was the only true statesman in Philip II's court. Mousset says that, for Longlée, "Seul Marc-Antoine Colonna a les qualités d'un homme de gouvernement" (p. xliii).
10. For example, Beatrice later says that he lent his heart "me awhile, and I

gave him use for it—a double heart for his single one. Marry, once before he won it of me with false dice" (2.1.249–51).

Chapter 10. What Rusts the Soul

1. Machiavelli's concept of the fox over the lion is developed in chapter 18 of *Il Principe*, "Quomodo fides a principibus sit servanda" (*Tutte le Opere di Niccolò Machiavelli*, ed. Francesco Flora and Carlo Cordiè, 2 vols. [Verona: Arnoldo Mondadori, 1949], 1: 55).

2. Bernard McElroy developed his idea in a paper entitled "The Private Lives of Public People: The Development of the Soliloquy in Shakespeare's English History Plays," delivered at the Central Renaissance Conference in Lawrence, Kans., April 1986.

3. Eugene Waith, "Manhood and Valor in *Macbeth*," *ELH* 17 (1950): 265–68, p. 267.

4. Walter Kaiser, ed., *Selected Essays in the Translation of John Florio*, Riverside Edition (Boston: Houghton Mifflin, 1964). Hereafter by page in text.

5. Cleanth Brooks, *The Well Wrought Urn* (New York: Harcourt Brace Jovanovitch, 1947), pp. 22–49.

6. Oscar James Campbell, "Shakespeare and the 'New Critics,'" from *Joseph Quincy Adams Memorial Studies*, ed. James G. McManaway, Giles E. Dawson, and Edwin E. Willoughby (Charlottesville: University of Virginia Press, 1948), pp. 85–91.

7. L. C. Knights, *Some Shakespearean Themes* (Stanford: Stanford University Press, 1959), pp. 14–19, 120–42. The above passages are all included in *Twentieth Century Interpretations of Macbeth*, ed. Terence Hawkes (Englewood Cliffs, N.J.: Prentice Hall, 1977).

8. "Porro mortalium vita omnis quid aliud est quam fabula quaepiam, in qua alii aliis obtecti personis procedunt aguntque suas quisque partes, donec choragus educat e proscenio?" In Desiderius Erasmus, *Opera Omnia* (Amsterdam: North Holland Publishing, 1969–), part 4, book 3, p. 104. I take *choragus* to mean stage "manager."

Chapter 11. Shakespeare's Critique of the Mirage of the Green World in *As You Like It* and *The Winter's Tale*

1. Hugh Richmond, *Shakespeare's Sexual Comedy: A Mirror for Lovers* (New York: Bobbs-Merrill, 1971), p. 205.

2. Dollimore, in *Radical Tragedy*, p. 49, notes, for example, Troilus's decline into warrior revenger. Bevington, in *Tudor Drama and Politics*, p. 240, suggests, Shakespeare "prejudicially" reports Cade's death and other circumstances of his activist career.

3. William Empson, *Some Versions of Pastoral* (London: Chatto and Windus, 1935), notably in chapter 1, "Proletarian Literature."

4. This concept of simultaneous pastoral and Edenic ideal jives with Sidney's notion of pastoral in the Defence of Poetry (94.33 to 95.11) as a means of condemning hierarchy ("dunghill") and hierarchical ambitions ("cock").

5. Sidney, *Miscellaneous Prose*, p. 96.

6. In the "Life of Cowley" and "Life of Milton," found in Samuel Johnson,

Lives of the English Poets, ed. George Birkbeck Hill (New York: Octagon, 1967), orig. Oxford: Clarendon, 1905, 3 vols. 1:1–69, 84–200, esp. 1:18–22, 163–165.

7. Weydemeyer, a follower of Marx in Rhenish Prussia, emigrated to the United States, eventually publishing Marx's masterpiece, *The Eighteenth Brumaire of Louis Bonaparte*, in the New York German paper *Die Revolution* of 1852. An abolitionist, he fought in the Civil War as a colonel in the Union forces. Until his death in 1868, he received a series of letters in which Marx updated his philosophical thinking. As an introduction to the Marxian problems I discuss, see Howard Selsam, David Goldway, and Harry Martel, eds., *Dynamics of Social Change: A Reader in Marxist Social Science* (New York: International Publishrs, 1970), where the famous letter to Weydemeyer is quoted briefly on p. 31.

8. Ernst Robert Curtius, *European Literature in the Latin Middle Ages*, trans. Willard Trask, Bollingen series 36 (New York: Pantheon, 1953), p. 85.

Chapter 12. Hierarchy and Freedom in the New World

1. In his epistle to the queen in 1591, as preface to his book *Of the Russe Commonwealth*, Giles Fletcher purports to present the "true and strange face of a Tyrannical State," opposed to that of English freedom. Persia become synonymous with autocracy. The queen in her speeches, notably at Tilbury in 1588, emphasized that "tyrannical" Spain was an un-English autocracy.

2. An interesting theatrical gloss to this discussion, suggested to me by Stephen Orgel, occurs in George Cukor's 1940 movie, *The Philadelphia Story*, adapted by Donald Ogden Stewart from the Philip Barry play of the same name. In it, the heroine, played by Katherine Hepburn, is regaling her edgy fiancé, played by John Howard, with a story about her first honeymoon on board a sailboat, called *The True Love*, she shared with her first husband, played by Cary Grant. When asked to describe the boat, she can only say it was "yar." Her businesslike fiancé having no idea what "yar" means, asks, and she responds airily, "Oh, smooth lines, quick to the helm, etc. etc." A gap in aesthetics and perhaps in class is, perhaps, here implied, but in Shakespeare the word seems an ordinary one, a sailor's term for whatever lends order and speed to a sailing ship, from halyard to "playing" of the men.

3. In his *The Cease of Majesty*, p. 147, M. M. Reese says:

> Even Prospero is implicitly censured for "neglecting worldly ends, all dedicated / To closeness and the bettering of my mind (Temp. 1 ii 89)," and Shakespeare suggests that these withdrawn and precious spirits are, in their contrasted way, just as much individualists, and so just as culpable politically, as men of violence like Richard III.

4. Although Shakespeare's paucity of female roles—probably predicated on the inevitable shortage of adolescent boys with suitable voices—forces some companies to give females male parts, Ariel's sex, I argue, however, must remain clearly male if the play is to remain coherent.

5. That sexual intercourse might be the referent here may help to explain the severity of Sycorax's punishment, that of a woman scorned.

6. Shakespeare's drama is replete with omens about retirement, voluntary or forced, though he retired early. After his son Hamnet died in 1596, he no doubt suspected that he would one day become a retiree with two marriageable daughters, Susanna and Judith, Hamnet's twin. The allure of freedom and

leisure in a town in the up-country, Stratford, however, never wholly eclipsed his involvement in London political and financial matters. Unlike King Lear, he did not suffer the consequences of either "abdication" or, like Duke Prospero, "enforced retirement." But the problem of the politics of retirement and freedom inspired his imagination, and after having more than touched on these problems in *As You Like It, King Lear, Timon of Athens, Anthony and Cleopatra, Pericles,* and other plays, in his semiretirement from about 1610, he produced his romance *The Tempest,* dwelling, in part, on Prospero's enforced retirement in a version of Atlantis.

7. The relationship of this passage to a utopian moment in Montaigne's "Des Cannibales" has often been discussed. Shakespeare again uses and subverts one of his masters by showing, once again, that when a well-oiled collective society requires a dictator, that state contradicts its own "collectivity." King Utopus or Gonzalo must be there to make it happen and preserve it from on high.

Epilogue. Ulysses' Political Thoughts and Action in Reverse

1. William Shakespeare, *Troilus and Cressida,* ed. Una Ellis-Fermor (London: Methuen, 1945), p. xxx.
2. See, for example, Dollimore's *Radical Tragedy,* pp. 40–50.
3. E. M. W. Tillyard, *The Elizabethan World Picture* (New York: Random House, n.d., orig. (New York: Macmillan, 1944), pp. 9–10, 16, 17, 25, 83, 88–89, 100.
4. Girard, *Violence and the Sacred,* trans. Patrick Gregory (Baltimore: Johns Hopkins University Press, 1977), p. 51.
5. Girard, *La Violence et le Sacré,* p. 80.
6. This position leads to readings of Shakespeare's comedy, somewhat like those of William Hazlitt, that may open the door to attacks on Girard's supposed "untheatrical" hermeneutics (see Harry Berger, Jr., "Text against Performance in Shakespeare: The Example of *Macbeth,*" in Stephen Greenblatt, ed., *The Forms of Power and the Power of Forms in the Renaissance,* a special edition of *Genre* 15 [1982]: 49–79, and Richard Levin, "The New Refutation of Shakespeare," *Modern Philology* 83 [1985]: 123–41). Without attempting to resolve that debate, I argue that Shakespeare, in *Troilus and Cressida* and elsewhere, creates a comic scapegoat and a comic version of the process that Girard discovers in the works of the master playwright. Shakespeare's comic object of ostracism, apparently, must perfectly deserve society's ganging up. Thus Shakespeare's central comic scapegoats, like Shylock and Malvolio, misuse the delicate legal system that would, if it functioned properly, make the scapegoat mechanism obsolete. In the Greek camp of the world of *Troilus and Cressida,* Thersites becomes a comic scapegoat in his use of language for the worse, words being the preservers of distinctions without which one might be forced to speak with hands, and people do. If Shakespeare's comic scapegoat exists, of course, leveling has a comic solution as well.

Bibliography

Albee, Edward. *Who's Afraid of Virginia Woolf?* New York: Atheneum, 1962.

Alpers, Paul J., ed. *Elizabethan Poetry: Modern Essays in Criticism.* Oxford: Oxford University Press, 1967.

Anderson, Peter S. "Shakespeare's *Caesar,* the Language of Sacrifice." *Comparative Drama* 3 (1969): 3–26.

Aubrey, John. *Aubrey's Brief Lives.* Edited by Oliver Lawson Dick. London: Secker & Warburg, 1960.

Barber, C. L. *Shakespeare's Festive Comedy: A Study of Dramatic Form and Its Relation to Social Custom.* Princeton: Princeton University Press, 1959.

Barish, Jonas. "The Prose Style of John Lyly." *ELH* 23 (1956): 14–35.

Berger, Harry, Jr. "Text against Performance in Shakespeare: The Example of *Macbeth.*" In *The Forms of Power and the Power of Forms in the Renaissance,* edited by Stephen Greenblatt, 49–79. *Genre* 15 (1982).

Berry, Ralph. "*Julius Caesar:* A Roman Tragedy." *Dalhousie Review* 61 (1981): 325–36.

Bevington, David. *Tudor Drama and Politics: A Critical Approach to Topical Meaning.* Cambridge: Harvard University Press, 1968.

Booth, Wayne. *The Rhetoric of Fiction.* Chicago: University of Chicago Press, 1961.

Brooks, Cleanth. *The Well-Wrought Urn: Studies in the Structure of Poetry.* New York: Reynal & Hitchcock, 1947.

Burke, Kenneth. "Antony in Behalf of the Play." In *The Philosophy of Literary Form: Studies in Symbolic Action,* 329–43. Baton Rouge: Louisiana State University Press, 1941.

Campbell, Oscar James. "Shakespeare and the 'New Critics.'" In *Joseph Quincy Adams Memorial Studies,* edited by James G. McManaway, Giles E. Dawson, and Edwin E. Willoughby, 85–91. Charlotteville: University of Virginia Press, 1948.

Chambers, R. W. "The Expression of Ideas—Particularly Political Ideas—in the Three Pages, and in Shakespeare." In *Shakespeare's Hand in the Play of Sir Thomas More,* edited by Alfred W. Pollard, 142–87. Cambridge: Cambridge University Press, 1923.

———. "Shakespeare and the Play of *More.*" In *Man's Unconquerable Mind,* 204–49. London: Jonathon Cape, 1939.

Curtius, Ernst Robert. *European Literature in the Latin Middle Ages.* Translated from the German by Willard Trask. Bollingen Series number 36. New York: Pantheon, 1953.

Dean, Leonard F., *Twentieth Century Interpretations of Julius Caesar.* Englewood Cliffs, N.J.: Prentice-Hall, 1968.

Dennis, John. *Critical Works*. Edited by Niles Hooker. 2 vols. Baltimore: Johns Hopkins University Press, 1939–43.

Dollimore, Jonathon. *Radical Tragedy: Religion, Ideology and Power in the Drama of Shakespeare and His Contemporaries*. Chicago: University of Chicago Press, 1984.

———, and Alan Sinfield, eds. *Political Shakespeare: New Essays in Cultural Materialism*. Ithaca: Cornell University Press, 1985.

Ebel, Henry. "Caesar's Wounds: A Study of William Shakespeare. *Psychoanalitic Review* 62 (1975): 107–30.

Empson, William. *Some Versions of Pastoral*. London: Chatto & Windus, 1935.

Erasmus, Desiderius. *Opera Omnia*. Amsterdam: North Holland Publishing, 1969–.

Evans, G. Blakemore. "The Problem of Brutus: An Eighteenth Century Solution." In *Studies in Honor of T. W. Baldwin*, edited by Don Cameron Allen, pp. 229–236. Urbana: University of Illinois Press, 1958.

Fineman, Joel. *Shakespeare's Perjured Eye: The Invention of Poetic Subjectivity in the Sonnets*. Berkeley: University of California Press, 1986.

Fletcher, Giles, Senior. *Of the Russe Common Wealth*. N.p. 1591.

Fly, Richard D. "'Suited in Like Conditions as Our Argument': Imitative Form in Shakespeare's *Troilus and Cressida*." *Studies in English Literature: 1500–1660* 15 (1975): 273–92.

Freud, Sigmund. *Moses and Monotheism*. Translated from the German by Katherine Jones. London: Hogarth Press, 1939.

———. *Totem and Taboo*. Vol. 13 of *The Standard Edition of the Complete Psychological Works*, edited and translated from the German by James Strachey. 24 vols. London: Hogarth Press, 1953–66.

Gerenday, Lynn de. "Play, Ritualization, and Ambivalence in *Julius Caesar*." *Literature and Psychology* 24 (1974): 24–34.

Girard, René. *La Violence et le Sacré*. Paris: Bernard Grasset, 1972. *Violence and the Sacred*. Translated from the French by Patrick Gregory. Baltimore: Johns Hopkins University Press, 1973.

Goddard, Harold C. *The Meaning of Shakespeare*. Chicago: University of Chicago Press, 1951.

Goldstein, Malcomb. "Pope, Sheffield, and Shakespeare's *Julius Caesar*." *Modern Language Notes* 71 (1956): 8–10.

Greenblatt, Stephen Jay. *Renaissance Self-Fashioning: From More to Shakespeare*. Chicago: University of Chicago Press, 1980.

———. *Shakespearean Negotiations: The Circulation of Social Energy in Renaissance England*. The New Historicism: Studies in Cultural Poetics, no. 4. Berkeley: University of California Press, 1988.

Greene, Robert. *Groats-VVorth of Witte, bought with a million of Repentence, 1592*. Edited by G. B. Harrison. Bodley Head quartos. London: E. P. Dutton, 1923.

Hawkes, Terrence, ed. *Twentieth Century Interpretations of Macbeth*. Englewood Cliffs, N.J.: Prentice-Hall, 1977.

Herrick, Marvin. *Comic Theory in the Sixteenth Century*. Urbana: University of Illinois Press, 1950.

Holland, Norman. "The 'Cinna' and 'Cynicke' Episodes in *Julius Caesar.*" *Shakespeare Quarterly* 11 (1960): 439–44.

Hume, Robert D. *The Development of English Drama in the Late Seventeenth Century.* Oxford: Clarendon, 1976.

Johnson, Samuel. *Johnson on Shakespeare.* Edited by Walter Raleigh. Oxford: Oxford University Press, 1908.

Jonson, Ben. *Ben Jonson.* Edited by C. H. Herford and Percy and Evelyn Simpson. 11 vols. Oxford: Clarendon, 1925–52.

———. *The Complete Poetry.* Edited by William B. Hunter, Jr. Anchor Books. Garden City, N.Y.: Doubleday, 1963.

———. *The Workes.* First Folio. London: William Stansby, 1616.

Kaula, David. "'Let Us Be Sacrificers': Religious Motifs in *Julius Caesar.*" *Shakespeare Studies* 14 (1981): 197–214.

Knight, G. Wilson. *The Imperial Theme: Further Interpretations of Shakespeare's Tragedies Including the Roman Plays.* Oxford University Press. London: Humphrey Milford, 1931.

Knights, L. C. *Explorations: Essays in Cirticism, Mainly on the Literature of the Seventeenth Century.* London: Chatto and Windus, 1946.

———. *Some Shakespearean Themes.* Stanford: Stanford University Press, 1959.

Koenigsburger, Helmut. *The Practice of Empire.* Ithaca: Cornell University Press, 1969.

Levao, Ronald. *Renaissance Minds and Their Functions: Casanus, Sidney, Shakespeare.* Berkeley: University of California Press, 1985.

Levin, Harry. "The Underplot of *Twelfth Night. De Shakespeare à T. S. Eliot: Melanges offerts à Henri Fluchére.* Edited by Marie-Jean Durry, Robert Ellrodt, and Marie Therese Jones-Davies, pp. 53–59. Etudes anglaises 63. Paris: Didier, 1976.

Levin, Richard. "The New Refutation of Shakespeare." *Modern Philology* 83 (1985): 123–41.

Liebler, Naomi Conn. "'Thou Bleeding Piece of Earth': The Ritual Ground of *Julius Caesar.*" *Shakespeare Studies* 14 (1981): 175–96.

Longlée, M. de. *Depêches Diplomatiques de M. de Longlée, Résident de France en Espagne (1582–1590).* Edited by Albert Mousset. Paris: Plon-Nourrit, 1912.

Lyly, John. *The Complete Works.* Edited by R. Warwick Bond. 3 vols. Oxford: Clarendon, 1902.

Machiavelli, Niccolo. *Tutte le Opere di Niccolo Machiavelli.* Edited by Francesco Flora and Carlo Cordiè. 2 vols. Verona: Arnoldo Mondadori, 1949.

Mack, Maynard. "Engagement and Detachment in Shakespeare's Play." In *Essays on Shakespeare and Elizabethan Drama in Honor of Hardin Craig,* edited by Richard Hasley, 275–96. Columbia: University of Missouri Press, 1962.

McMillan Scott. *The Elizabethan Theatre and "The Book of Sir Thomas More."* Ithaca: Cornell University Press, 1987.

Marlowe, Christopher. *The Complete Works.* Edited by Fredson Bowers. 2 vols. Cambridge: Cambridge University Press, 1973.

Marx, Karl. *The Eighteenth Brumaire of Louis Bonaparte.* Edited and translated from the German by C. P. Dutt. New York: International Publishers, 1963.

Matchett, William H. "Shylock, Iago, and *Sir Thomas More:* With Some Further Discussion of Shakespeare's Imagination." *PMLA* 92 (1977): 217–30.

Montaigne, Michel de. *Selected Essays in the Translation of John Florio.* Edited by Walter Kaiser. Riverside edition. Boston: Houghton Mifflin, 1964.

Mueschke, Paul, and Jeanette Fleisher. "Jonsonian Elements in the Comic Underplot of *Twelfth Night.*" *PMLA* 48 (1933): 722–40.

Ornstein, Robert. *Shakespeare's Comedies: From Roman Force to Romantic Mystery.* Newark: University of Delaware Press, 1986.

Patterson, Annabel. *Censorship and Interpretation: The Conditions of Writing and Reading in Early Modern England.* Madison: University of Wisconsin Press, 1984.

Perkins, William. *The Workes.* 3 vols. London: John Haviland, 1631.

Plutarch. *Lives.* Translated by Thomas North. Edited by W. E. Henley and George Windham. 6 vols. London: David Nut, 1895.

Rabkin, Norman. "Common Characteristics of Brutus and Caesar." *Journal of English and Germanic Philology* 63 (1964): 240–54.

———. *Shakespeare and the Common Understanding.* New York: Free Press, 1967.

Reese, M. M. *The Cease of Majesty: A Study of Shakespeare's History Plays.* London: Edward Arnold, 1961.

"Remarks upon the Tragedy of *Julius Caesar.*" *British Magazine* 8 (1767): 571–74.

Richmond, Hugh. *Shakespeare's Political Plays.* New York: Random House, 1967.

———. "Shakespeare's Roman Trilogy: The Climax in *Cymbeline.*" *Studies in the Literary Imagination* 5 (1972): 129–40.

———. *Shakespeare's Sexual Comedy: A Mirror for Lovers.* New York: Bobbs-Merrill, 1971.

Riggs, David. *Shakespeare's Heroical Histories: "Henry VI" and Its Literary Tradition.* Cambridge: Harvard University Press, 1971.

Rossiter, A. P. *Angel with Horns: And Other Shakespeare Lectures.* Edited by Graham Storey. New York: Theatre Arts Books, 1961.

Rothstein, Eric. *Restoration Tragedy: Form and the Process of Change.* Madison: University of Wisconsin Press, 1967.

Rymer, Thomas. *The Critical Works.* Edited by Curt A. Zimansky. New Haven: Yale University Press, 1956.

Saccio, Peter. "Shrewd and Kindly Farce." *Shakespeare Survey: An Annual Survey of Shakespearian Study and Production* 37 (1984): 33–40.

Schoenbaum, S. *William Shakespeare: A Compact Documentary Life.* New York: Oxford University Press, 1977.

Seligman, Kevin L. "Shakespeare's Use of Elizabethan Dress as a Comedic Device in *The Taming of the Shrew:* 'Something Mechanical Encrusted on the Living.'" *Quarterly Journal of Speech* 60 (1964): 39–44.

Selsam, Howard, David Goldway, and Harry Martel, ed. *Dynamics of Social Change: A Reader in Marxist Social Science.* New York: International Publishers, 1970.

Shakespeare, William. *The Complete Pelican Shakespeare*. Edited by Alfred Harbage. Baltimore: Penguin, 1969.

———. *Hamlet*. Edited by Horace Howard Furness. New Variorum Edition. 2 vols. Philadelphia: J. Lippincott, 1905.

———. *Julius Caesar*. Edited by T. S. Dorsch. Arden edition. London: Methuen, 1955.

———. *Shakespeare's Sonnets*. Edited and commented upon by Stephen Booth. New Haven: Yale University Press, 1977.

———. *The Taming of the Shrew*. Edited by Robert B. Heilman. In *The Complete Signet Classic Shakespeare*, edited by Silvan Barnet. New York: Harcourt Brace Jovanovich, 1972.

———. *Troilus and Cressida*. Edited by Una Ellis-Fermor. Arden edition. London: Methuen, 1945.

———. *The Works of Shakespeare in Six Volumes*. Edited by Alexander Pope. London: Jacob Tonson, 1725.

Sheffield, John. *The Tragedy of Julius Caesar. Altered*. In *The Works of John Sheffield, Duke of Buckingham*. 2 vols. London: John Barber. 1723.

Sidney, Sir Philip. *The Miscellaneous Prose*. Edited by Katherine Duncan-Jones and Jan Van Dorsten. Oxford: Clarendon, 1973.

———. *The Poems of Sir Philip Sidney*. Edited by William A. Ringler, Jr. Oxford: Clarendon Press, 1968.

Siemon, James R. *Shakespearean Iconoclasm*. Berkeley: University of California Press, 1985.

Stirling, Brents. "Or Else Were This a Savage Spectacle." *PMLA* 66 (1951): 765–74.

———. *Unity in Shakespearian Tragedy*. New York: Columbia University Press, 1956.

Strier, Richard, and Heather Dubrow, eds. *The Historical Renaissance: New Essays in Tudor and Stuart Literature and Culture*. Chicago: University of Chicago Press, 1988.

Taylor, Gary, and Michael Warren, eds. *The Division of Kingdoms: Shakespeare's Two Versions of King Lear*. Oxford: Clarendon, 1983.

Tillyard, E. M. W. *The Elizabethan World Picture*. New York: Random House, n.d., orig. New York: Macmillan, 1944.

———. *Shakespeare's Early Comedies*. New York: Barnes & Noble, 1965.

———. *Shakespeare's History Plays*. New York: Macmillan, 1946.

Velz, John W. *Shakespeare and the Classical Tradition: A Critical Guide to Commentary, 1660–1960*. Minneapolis: University of Minnesota Press, 1968.

———, comp. *The Tragedy of Julius Caesar: A Bibliography to Supplement the New Variorum Edition of 1913*. New York: Modern Language Association, 1977.

Waith, Eugene. "Manhood and Valor in *Macbeth*." *ELH* 17 (1950): 265–68.

Wentersdorf, Karl P. "Linkages of Thought and Imagery in Shakespeare and More." *Modern Language Quarterly* 34 (1973): 384–405.

Whitaker, Tina. *Sicily through the Ages*. New York: Dutton, 1926.

Wilson, John Dover. "Ben Jonson and 'Julius Caesar'" *Shakespeare Survey* 2 (1949): 36–43.

Yeats, William Butler. *Essays and Introductions*. New York: Macmillan, 1961.

Index

Ad hominem argument, 93
Aesop, 97
Albee, Edward, 146 n.9
Alchemist (Ben Jonson), 79, 147 n.19
Anderson, Peter S., 143 n.2
Anthropological themes, 143 n.2
Antigone (Sophocles), 117
Antony and Cleopatra, 58, 62, 151–52 n.6
Aristotle, 11, 25, 140 n.15
Armstrong, Edward A., 42
As You Like It, 45, 69 151–52 n.6; mirage of green world in, 117–26
Aubrey, John, 93, 149 n.5
Autocratic concept, 11, 41–44, 127–33, 139 n.3

Bacon, Francis, 12, 105
Baited bear, image of, 77, 81, 86
"Banquo" and "banquet," wordplay on, 109–10
Barber, C. L., 146 n.5
Barish, Jonas, 146 n.10 (chap. 6)
Barry, Philip, 151 n.2
Beckett, Thomas à, 97
Benevolent deception, 14, 21–38, 105–14, 135–38
Bergson, Henri, 141 n.2
Berry, Ralph, 144 n.2
Bevington, David, 10, 41–42, 44, 117, 145 n.10, 150 n.2 (chap. 11)
"Black" Machiavellian interpretation, 140 n.1
Blood, image of, 51, 108, 111–12
Boils and plague, image of, 46
Booth, Stephen, 13, 21, 25
Booth, Wayne, 79
Borgia, Cesare, 26
Brainwashing, 27, 29, 30
Breeding, concept of, 27–28
Brooks, Cleanth, 109
Brown, Thomas, 149 n.2

Burke, Kenneth, 143 n.2
Bush, Douglas, 24

Campbell, Oscar James, 109
Candor, 27
Cannibalism, 42, 47–48, 102–3
Catachresis, 71
Catiline (Ben Jonson), 90
Chambers, R. W., 41, 43, 44; image of "knees as feet," 46
Chaos, 127
Characters: female, 130, 151 n.4; practice of thrusting identifies on, 142 n.6
Charisma: development of, 35; explanation of political, in sonnet 94, 22
Charismatic leadership, 9
Christian archetypes, occult references to, 143 n.2
Cicero, 91
Civil disturbance, 41–57
Civilizing, 27
Coke, Sir Edward, 139 n.3
Coleridge, Samuel Taylor, 147 n.19
Collective ideal, 14, 45, 63, 117–26
Collective violence, 11–12, 41–58, 88–94, 135–38
Colonna, Marc Antonio, 99–100, 149 n.9
Comedy of Errors, 100
Confidence games, 81, 83
Conscience, invention of, and Macbeth, 105–14
Conspiracy, conflict between idealism and, 10
Contagion: image of, 46; metaphor of, in *Julius Caesar*, 54
Control, Brutus's angst about, 9
Coriolanus, 41, 43, 49; choice of attire in, 45; "contagion" in, 46; image of "boils and plagues" in, 46; justice

system in, 49; "leveling" of clothing in, 45
Corruption, 25
Cosa nostra, 97
Cowley, Abraham, 118
Cukor, George, 151 n.2
Curtius, Ernst Robert, 121
Cymbeline, 58, 122

Daniel, Samuel, 12, 68
David, 50
Decay, theme of, 144 n.2
Dennis, John, 90
Devil, image of, 113, 139–40 n.6
De Vita Caesarum (Suetonius), 92
Dis-ease, 35, 38, 94, 107
Disjunction, use of, to symbolize disorder, 42
Dog, 144 n.4
Dollimore, Jonathon, 12, 42, 117, 140 n.9, 150 n.2 (chap. 11)
Doria, Andrea, 149 n.9
Dorsch, T. S., 148 n.10
Double, 78, 123
Drummond, William, 78
Dryden, John, 147 n.2
Duchess of Malfi (John Webster), 117

Ebel, Henry, 143–44 n.2
Education, Shakespeare on, 26–33
Egoism, 27; perils of, 117
Elizabeth I (England), 98; dangers on potential retirement of, 10
Elizabethan policies, poetic criticisms of, 50
Ellis-Fermor, Una, 135
Empson, William, 117, 140 n.1, 141 n.7
Encomium Moriae (Erasmus), 33
England, link between Sicily and, 97–104
Epicureanism, 63
Equalizing, 10
Erasmus, Desiderius, 33, 150 n.8
Ethnic restraint, 25
Ethnos and *ethos*, 12, 144 n.2
Euphues: The Anatomy of Wit (John Lyly), 74
Euphuism, 68, 72–75
Evans, G. Blakemore, 148 n.16
Every Man in His Humour (Ben Jonson), 76, 79

Every Man Out of His Humour (Ben Jonson), 92
Exorcism, 77, 80–81
Exposure of children, 124–25

Factional behavior, Shakespearean concept of, 41–50
Family, political locale of, 27–28
Female roles, 130, 151 n.4
Fineman, Joel, 26
Fire, image of, 46
Fleisher, Jeanette, 76
Fletcher, Giles, 10, 139 n.3, 151 n.1
Flood, image of, 43–44, 46, 53
Florio, John, 106–7
Flower, image of, 24–25
Fly, Richard, 42
Ford, John, 117
Foreconceit, 13
Foucault, Michel, 25
Fox, deception of, 106
Fox over the lion, concept of, 150 n.1 (chap. 10)
Freedom, English guarantees of, 10
Freud, Sigmund, 143 n.2
"Freudian" ambivalence, 144 n.2

Gallantry, critique of, in *Much Ado about Nothing*, 97–104
Geck, image of, 86
Gerenday, Lynn de, 144 n.2
Girard, René, 11, 13, 135–36, 143 n.11
Goddard, Harold C., 141 n.4
Goldstein, Malcomb, 148 n.22
Grace, theological concept of, 23
Greenblatt, Stephen, 12–13, 42, 140 n.9, 141 n.8
Greene, Robert, 14, 68, 100, 145 n.4
Green world, mirage of, in *As You Like It* and *Winter's Tale*, 117–26
Gregory, Patrick, 135
Greville, Fulke, 105
Gull, 80–82, 86, 147 nn. 12 and 13
Gull-catching, 77, 146 n.6
Gull-victimization, 77

Hamartia, 148 n.19
Hamlet, 69, 90, 106, 128; conscience in, 107–8
Hazlitt, William, 152 n.6
Heilman, Robert B., 141 n.5
Henriad, 27, 142 n.2 (chap. 3); idioms

INDEX

in, 67
1 *Henry IV*, 34–38; Lyly and Marlowe in, 67–75; concept of honor in, 37
Henry V, 105; benevolent deception and rule in, 34–38; concept of Machiavellian "hypocrite" ruler in, 27
2 *Henry VI*, 41, 44, 46, 49; image of fire in, 46; justice system in, 48, 49
Henry VIII, Renaissance court of, 33
Herbarist imagery, 74
Hermeneutics, 152 n.6
Hero and Leander (Christopher Marlowe), 69
Herrick, Marvin, 146 n.5
Holland, Norman, 143 n.2
Honor, concept of, 37, 67–75, 88, 97–104, 148 n.11
Howard, John, 151 n.2
Hyperbole, 71

Iconoclasm, 12
Idealism, 14; conflict between conspiracy and, 10; Shakespearean staging of, 117–26
Idioms, in the *Henriad*, 67
"Ill May Day Scene," speech of Sir Thomas More in, 41, 43, 49–50
Il Principe (Machiavelli), 26
Image cluster, 43, 44
Imagination, Shakespearean concept of, 42
Improvisation, Shakespearean versions of, 141 n.8
Irene (Samuel Johnson), 89
Irony, in sonnet 94, 21

Johnson, Samuel, 89, 92, 118–19
Jonson, Ben, 14, 75, 76–87, 89, 90, 92, 146 n.9 (chap. 6), 2, 4, and 6
Judicial parody, in *Julius Caesar*, 48–49
Julius Caesar, 41, 43, 48, 49, 50, 67, 75; choice of attire in, 44–45; dismembering text in early criticism of, 88–94; images of storms and plagues in, 46; judicial parody in, 48–49; leveling in, 38, 51–53, 88–89; role of Brutus in, 9–10; unrecognizable clothing of crowd in, 45, 52–53; world of horror in, 14
Justice: in *Coriolanus*, 49; in 2 *Henry VI*, 48, 49; in *Troilus and Cressida*, 49

Kaula, David, 144 n.2
Killigrew, T., 93
King Lear, 13, 90, 118, 151–52 n.6; leveling in, 51
Knees as feet, image of, 46, 47–48
Knight, G. Wilson, 51
Knights, L. C., 21, 109
Koenigsberger, Helmut, 98–99
Kyd, Thomas, 14, 68

Latten spoon, 90–91
L'Estrange, Nicholas, 90
Levao, Ronald, 139 n.5
Leveling, 9, 11–13, 63, 114, 136; in *Julius Caesar*, 38, 51–53, 88, 112; in *King Lear*, 51; in *Macbeth*, 105–14; Shakespearean interpretation of, 41–50, 67
Levin, Harry, 146 n.5
Lévi-Strauss, Claude, 143 n.2
Liebler, Naomi Conn, 144 n.2
Literary expropriation, politics of, 67–75
Lonely words, Shakespeare's sophisticated use of, 106
Love, image of, 51, 117–20
Lucentio-Bianca plot, 31
Luciferian faction, 11
Lupercal, 53, 61, 94, 144 n.4
Lycidas (John Milton), 118
Lyly, John, 12, 14, 72–75; Shakespearean link with Christopher Marlowe, 68

Macbeth, 50, 90, 94, 118; concept of Machiavellian "hypocrite" ruler in, 27; and the invention of conscience, 105–14; world of horror in, 14
McElroy, Bernard, 150 n.2 (chap. 10)
Machiavelli, 11, 26–27
Machiavellian political doctrine, 21–25
Machiavellian ruler, concept of, in sonnet 94, 21–25
Machismo, 81–87, 101–4
Mack, Maynard, 142 n.6
McMillin, Scott, 142 n.1 (chap. 4)
Magna Carta, 10, 139 n.3
Malevolent deception, 25

Mano nera, 97
Marlovian blank verse, 71–72
Marlowe, Christopher, 12, 14, 69–72; Shakespearean link with John Lyly, 68
Marx, Karl, 119, 120–21, 151 n.7
Matchett, William, 42, 43
Menenius Agrippa, as consummate artist, 50
Merchant of Venice, 72, 151–52 n.6
"Metal," wordplay on, 60, 144–45 n.8
Milton, John, 33, 118, 139 n.3
"Mine," wordplay based on, 101–2
Monarchs, dangers of self-deposition of, 139 n.4
Montaigne, Michel de, 106–7, 112–14; on corrosive effect of lying, 33
More, Sir Thomas, speech of, in "Ill May Day Scene," 49–50
Much Ado about Nothing, 94, 117–18, 122; critique of gallantry in, 97–104
Mueschke, Paul, 76
Mutability, 59
Mysteries, sacrificing of, in early criticism of *Julius Caesar*, 88–94

"Naked new-born babe," significance of, 109
Nathan, 50
Nature, theological concept of, 23
New world, hierachy and freedom in, 127–34

Onomatopoeic alliteration, 69
Orgel, Stephen, 151 n.2
Ornstein, Robert, 141 n.1
Ostracism, 152 n.6
Othello, 90, 106, 122, 128

Parliamentarian traditions, 10, 97–104, 127, 139 n.3
Pastoral, as term, 117, 150 n.4 (chap. 11)
Pastoral ideal, 118–19, 120
Patterson, Annabel, 13, 143 n.14
Perfectibility, Icarian nature of schemes of, 14
Pericles, 76, 151–52 n.6
Perkins, William, 139 n.6
Pharmakos, 92, 144 n.4
"Pheese," interpretations of, 141 n.5
Philip II (Spain), 98, 99, 149 n.9

Plague: image of, 46; metaphor of, in *Julius Caesar*, 54, 88; metaphor of, in *Troilus and Cressida*, 46
Plebeians, rebellion of, 43–44
Plutarch, 90, 144 n.4, 149 n.23
Poetic justice, 86, 90, 94
Poetic rivalry, in Shakespearean sonnets, 67
Polansky, Roman, 109
Political theory, in sonnet 94, 25
Pompey, murder of, 57–58
Pope, Alexander, 94, 148 n.22
Primitive sacrificial customs, in *Julius Caesar*, 51

Rabkin, Norman, 145 n.10
Rationis capax, 11
Realpolitik, 27
Reese, M. M., 37, 128–28, 142 n.2 (chap. 3), 151 n.3
Religious motifs, 144 nn. 2 and 4
Renaissance political theoreticians, 11
Renaissance self-fashioning, 12
Restoration tragedy, 90
Restoration tragic theory, 90
Retirement, 151 n.6
Revenge tragedy, 62
Rich, Barnabe, 79
Richard Coeur de Lion, 97
Richmond, Hugh, 56, 117
Ritual gathering, ambivalence of, 51–52
Ritual imagery, 144 n.4
Ritual observance, 47
Ritual sacrifice, 47–48, 48, 89
Rival poets, idiom of, 68
Rivalry, 13, 51, 58–61, 67, 70–71, 75–76, 86–87, 90–91, 100–104, 108, 123–25, 135–38
Romance-plot motifs, 79
Romeo and Juliet, 117–19, 145 n.9
Rossiter, A. P., 34, 141 n.7
Rothstein, Eric, 90
Rule, 13; hypocrisy of, 35; problem of, 12; Shakespearean concept of, 25
Rymer, Thomas, 63, 90, 93, 147 n.2

Saccio, Peter, 141 n.1
Sacrifice: failed, in *Julius Caesar*, 51–53; Shakespeare's use of, 88–94, 143–44 n.2

Index

Satisfaction, 148 n.11
Saturnalian ritual imagery, 144 n.4
Savagery, Bianca's version of, 31–32
Savage spectacle, as leitmotif, 51
Scapegoat, 37–38, 42, 46, 51, 56, 63, 67, 77, 86, 88–94, 135, 136, 138, 143 n.2, 144 n.4, 152 n.6
Scapegoat spectacle, 11
Sejanus (Ben Jonson), 89
Seligman, Kevin L., 141 n.2
Shakespeare, William: concept of education, 26–33; imitation of John Lyly's antithetical style, 72–73; political stance of, 41
Shakespearean tragicomedy, 104
"Shaking scenes," 69
Sheffield, John, 93–94, 148 nn. 19 and 22
"Sicilian Vespers," 149 n.6
Sicily, link between England and, 97–104
Sidney, Sir Philip, 12, 13, 50, 70, 73, 105, 139 nn. 3 and 4, 143 n.13
Siemon, James, 13
Sir Clyomon and Clamydes (anon.), 79
Sir Thomas More, 41, 43, 46; image of plague and unnamed infection in, 46
Sly, Christopher, 28, 29, 30
Social order, Shakespearean view of, 33
Soellner, Rolf, 142 n.8
Sonnet 93, 21
Sonnet 94, 26, 34; benevolent deception and rule in, 21–25; "call" and "answer" of, 35; concept of Machiavellian ruler in, 21–25
Sonnet 95, 21
Sophocles, 117
Spenser, Edmund, 12
Stage, concept of world as, 114
Staple of News (Ben Jonson), 148 n.10
Stewart, Donald Ogden, 24, 151 n.2
Stirling, Brents, 51
Stoicism, 54, 63, 94
Strier, Richard, 13
Suetonius, 91, 92, 149 n.23

Tamburlaine (Christopher Marlowe), 117
Taming, concept of, 27

Taming of the Shrew, 105; benevolent deception and rule in, 34–38; Shakespearean concept of education in, 26–33
Tate, Nahum, 90
Tempest, 76, 114, 120, 127, 151–52 n.6
Temptation, 22–23
Terrestrial paradise, 125
Thersites, 152 n.6
Thought or image cluster, 42
Tillyard, E. M. W., 67, 68, 135, 142 n.6, 145 n.1, 146 n.10 (chap. 6)
Timber: or Discoveries (Ben Jonson), 92, 148 n.10
'Tis Pity She's a Whore (John Ford), 117
Tragedy of Dido, Queen of Carthage (Christopher Marlowe), 69
Troilus and Cressida, 41, 42, 135, 152 n.6; justice system in, 49; legal system in, 49; mask in, 45
Tropes, 71
Tudor myth, 145 n.1
Twelfth Night, 75; exorcizing Jonsonian citizen comedy in, 76–87

Ulysses, 41; analysis of political troubles in *Troilus and Cressida*, 41; deconstruction and reconstruction of notion of political process, 14; on floods, 46; political thoughts and actions of, in reverse, 135–38
"Under the Greenwood Tree," 45, 118, 122
Undiscoverable identity, problem of, in *Julius Caesar*, 53–54
University Wits, 68
Utopian activism, 117
Utopian collective ideal, 45

Velz, John W., 148 n.8
Vendetta, 62, 97, 99, 102, 148 n.11
Victimization, 13
Volpone (Ben Jonson), 79–82, 84–85
Vraisemblance, 77

Waith, Eugene, 106
Walter of England, 97
Webster, John, 117
Websterian tragedy, 100, 104
Weed, 25

Wentersdorf, Karl P., 43
Weydemeyer, Joseph, 120–21, 151 n.7
Whitaker, Tina, 97
White lie, Shakespearean use of metaphor of, 32
"White" Machiavellian interpretation, 21–25, 140 n.1
Will, ritual observance of unanimity of, 47
William of Orange, 149 n.9
Winter's Tale, 76, 98, 100, 114; mirage of green world in, 117–26
Wolf, image of, 53
Wordplay: on "Banquo" and "banquet," 109–10; on "metal," "mettle," "Metellus," "meddle," and "melt," 60, 144–45 n.8; on "mine," 101–2; on "Percy" and "pierce him," 75
World, concept of, as stage, 114

"Yare," 127–34
Yeats, William Butler, 142 n.3 (chap. 3)

Zeffirelli, Franco, 28